HOLLOWAY PRISON
The Place and the People

By the same author

Bellringing

HOLLOWAY PRISON

The Place and the People

JOHN CAMP

DAVID & CHARLES

NEWTON ABBOT   LONDON

NORTH POMFRET (VT)   VANCOUVER

ISBN 0 7153 6764 1
Library of Congress Catalog Card Number 74 19801
© John Camp 1974

Set in 11 on 13 point Baskerville
and printed in Great Britain
by John Sherratt & Son Ltd
for David & Charles (Holdings) Limited
South Devon House Newton Abbot Devon

Published in the United States of America
by David & Charles Inc   North Pomfret
Vermont 05053 USA

Published in Canada by Douglas David &
Charles Limited 3645 McKechnie Drive
West Vancouver BC

CONTENTS

LIST OF ILLUSTRATIONS

FOREWORD

Holloway Prison, in North London, has always fascinated me.
As a child, living within the area bounded by Camden
and Holloway Road, I took every opportunity of exploring the
district. I revelled in the shops and the never-ending traffic at
the Nag's Head, where the 'new' road from Camden Town to
Finsbury crossed the ancient highway which vanished north-
wards towards the mysterious regions of Kentish Town and
Highgate.

Through the line of trees marking the junction of Parkhurst
and Camden Roads one could catch a glimpse of the fairy-tale
tower and battlemented walls of Britain's biggest women's
prison. In my youthful imagination it became a castle peopled
with damsels in distress all awaiting rescue, for it was difficult
to believe that this extraordinary building was in reality a
penitentiary. But the greatest thrill of all was to take a ride
on an open-top bus which, conveniently but tactlessly, stopped
immediately outside the prison gates. From there one could
catch a glimpse of the secret and mysterious world within the
walls and see the endless rows of barred windows which so
effectively brought one back to grim reality.

Now the prison, with its crenellated towers and bizarre
architecture, is doomed. A famous London landmark which

9

has existed for well over a century is to vanish forever, and there will be few to mourn it. On the site a new Holloway is rising, clinical and self-sufficient, its functional steel and concrete buildings grouped around a wide, green campus as different in concept from Holloway's mock castle as the original prison was from Newgate or Millbank in its own day.

Will there be ghosts in the new Holloway? Shall we, perhaps, catch the sound of a sigh as Oscar Wilde, with tear-stained face, tries to talk to 'Bosie' Douglas on his daily visit? Will the quiet of the night be disturbed by the anguished cries of the suffragettes as tubes are forced down throats and into nostrils in the degrading torture of forcible feeding? Will the frail form of Edith Thompson, probably Holloway's most pathetic victim, haunt the campus by moonlight as a reminder of what many consider to be one of the greatest miscarriages of British justice? Or will Ruth Ellis, the last woman to be hanged in Britain, return to tell a new generation of the false and brittle values of a post-war London which she never really understood, and which destroyed her as surely as Hitler's bombs crushed the city?

Probably not. Those whose cries have echoed round the lofty iron cage of Holloway will have no wish to return. Perhaps their memory will live in the minds of those responsible for the new prison, and they will profit from the mistakes and inhumanities of the past imposed by a well-meaning but misguided administration.

Whether or not prison is the solution to the treatment of delinquency will long be argued, and there are many who wish to see custodial treatment abolished for all but the most grave offences. They may well be right. But, in the meantime, prisons remain the pivot of our penal system and, as is so often true of critics, their alternatives are far from convincing. Those concerned with the administration of prisons and the welfare of offenders have to endeavour to ensure that the regulations of the Home Office are always implemented, but with as much humanity and understanding as is consistent with discipline.

The new Holloway, in its design and concept, represents a new attitude to women in prison. It should go far to improving the lot of the prisoner while in custody and, even more importantly, alter her attitude to life when released. We can hope that it also represents the shape of things to come in the prison system generally. But in the meantime too many of our older prisons remain. Pentonville, Brixton, Wandsworth, Dartmoor, Strangeways and many other prisons up and down the country, some older and more antiquated than Holloway, are still in daily use.

JOHN CAMP
Wingrave, Buckinghamshire, 1974

I

THE BACKGROUND

No history or description of a Victorian prison can be attempted
without at least a brief consideration of penal development
during the preceding century. The Victorian era, with its
emerging social conscience, its burgeoning industrial capacity
and its rapid advances in transport and communication, seems
a world away from the conditions which applied in eighteenth-
century England. The discoveries and inventions that marked
the nineteenth century brought unheard-of benefits to the mass
of the population and those who brought them about are deeply
etched in the history of the times and unlikely to be forgotten.
Men like Stephenson, Brunel, Lister, Davy and Telford blazed
a trail the results of which we take for granted today.

Less spectacular, and largely overshadowed by such giants,
were those who worked for the improvement of social conditions at the turn of the century. For them the way was hard,
and public conscience was to be slow in awakening. Few
received their share of publicity in their lifetime and, for those
who did, it was too often coupled with suspicion and hostility.

Whilst those who worked amongst the poor were suspect,
infinitely more dangerous, according to eighteenth-century
standards, were those who concerned themselves with the fate

13

of felons and wrongdoers. Few were determined or brave enough to attempt it.

Prison conditions until the beginning of the nineteenth century were primitive and barbaric. In theory under the control of the local authority, most prisons were leased to private individuals as a business venture, the profits to the lessees represented by the amounts that could be extorted from the wretched inmates, who were expected to pay for the doubtful privilege of confinement in prison. Men, women and children were housed indiscriminately in buildings that never saw the light of day, that were never cleaned and which created a breeding-ground for typhus, the dreaded 'gaol fever' that carried off hundreds of prisoners long before their sentences were completed. Those with no money languished and starved in squalor; those with any resources at all were forced to pay extortionate sums for extra food and what sparse comfort could be obtained. Many a prisoner, having served his sentence, was forced to remain in gaol through inability to pay the sums supposedly due to the proprietor.

There were few to worry about the fate of prisoners. One man who did, however, was John Howard, a wealthy country squire from Bedfordshire who, in 1775, was appointed High Sheriff of the county. In this capacity he was required to inspect the prisons and penitentiaries in his area, and what he found appalled him. A widower, with little to occupy him at home, John Howard determined to devote the rest of his life to the amelioration of prison conditions. For almost twenty years he travelled widely, both in Britain and abroad, writing about his findings and constantly endeavouring to arouse both in the public conscience and in that of Parliament a realisation of the urgency of the matter. He campaigned for improved hygiene and sanitation; for the segregation of the sexes in prison; and for the classification of prisoners according to sentence and degree of crime. But most of all, Howard was concerned that the system of 'private' prisons should be abolished, and that prison staff should be paid out of the county rate and not be dependent on what could be extracted from prisoners.

By the time Howard died on a visit to Russia in 1790, Parliament was becoming aware of his views and was beginning to take them seriously. Agitation for a change in the system passed to others, including the redoubtable Elizabeth Fry, a Quaker, and Jeremy Bentham, whose ideas on prison architecture were eventually to bear fruit. Eventually the Government was persuaded that prison reform was long overdue, though it was to be many years before all Howard's recommendations were finally accepted.

The accession of Queen Victoria in 1837 coincided with a determined effort by Parliament to improve the conditions applying in prisons in England and Wales. Two years earlier, in 1835, a nationwide survey had investigated the matter and an Act had been passed by which Government inspectors of prisons had been appointed for the first time. In 1839 a new Prison Act made recommendations regarding the separation of prisoners 'in order to prevent contamination', and imposed rules on their treatment according to their classification.

One of the main difficulties associated with prison administration during the early years of the nineteenth century was that prisons did not come under a central authority, but were administered by local authorities whose ideas on the subject varied enormously. The creation of prison inspectors in 1835 had been an attempt to impose greater uniformity in such matters as diet, exercise, work whilst in prison, punishment and general prison security. Though the work of the inspectors was to provide Westminster with a much more accurate picture of prison life than had been possible before (until 1835 the Government did not even know exactly how many prisons existed), it was quite another matter to persuade local authorities to accept these recommendations.

The issue that created most dissension was the policy of

'cellular' confinement, a move away from the free association of prisoners, men and women, old and young, that had been condemned by Elizabeth Fry and John Howard. It was obvious that a system of individual cells for prisoners would mean the virtual rebuilding of most prisons, something which few local authorities were willing to undertake, and which was not seriously tried until the opening of Pentonville in 1842.

In London the situation was complicated by the fact that several local authorities whose boundaries converged on the metropolis had prisons in the area, and some other prisons were directly under the control of the Home Office. The Government, which had at last taken note of the recommendations of Howard, began to put its own house in order when it opened an immense new penitentiary on Millbank in 1812. Built on the cellular system, this prison had accommodation for 600, and was intended to house convicts sentenced to transportation, for periods of three to five years before their eventual departure to Gibraltar, Bermuda or Australia. Alterations and improvements, long overdue, were also made to the ancient Newgate Prison, and in 1817 Elizabeth Fry and her Quaker friends were allowed to form a Ladies' Prison Committee in an attempt to improve the conditions of the female convicts.

It had been hoped that the opening of Millbank would eventually allow Newgate to be closed. Unfortunately, as the prison population refused to diminish, it became apparent that not only would Newgate continue in use but that at least one more large prison would soon be required for the London area. In the meantime improvements were being made to existing prisons, and a system instituted allocating certain classes of prisoners to specific prisons.

By 1841 the prison accommodation available in London was as follows:

Newgate (1785): Men, women and boys, convicted and on remand.

Coldbath Fields (1794): Adult males.

Millbank (1812): Men and women serving sentences prior to transportation.

Horsemonger Lane (1816): Men and women, including debtors.

Clerkenwell (1820): Men and women on remand and waiting trial.

Brixton (1822): Women and girls.

Tothill Fields (1836): Convicted men and boys, men and women on remand, debtors.

Additional prison accommodation had been provided since 1776 in three disused hulks moored in the Thames off Woolwich.

Civil prisoners were housed as follows:

Fleet Prison: Debtors and those guilty of contempt of court.

Marshalsea: Debtors.

King's Bench Prison: Those guilty of libel or slander.

All three were closed in 1841, and debtors were lodged in a temporary prison in Whitecross Street.

In 1842 London's latest and most advanced prison was built by the Government in the Caledonian Road. This was Pentonville, the 'New Model Prison' whose design was to remain a prototype of English prisons until the building of Wormwood Scrubs in 1874. Pentonville was the first prison in London to be built on the new radial principle. Several blocks of cells radiated from a central circular building, the object being that prison officers situated in this building could have an uninterrupted view down the corridors of each wing on any floor. The principle of cellular confinement had been advocated by John Howard and his contemporary, Sir William Blackstone, and had been the subject of an Act of Parliament in 1778. But as already commented, nothing came of this at the time. In 1837 the then Secretary of State to the Home Department had recommended the system to the magistracy for their consideration. Pentonville was the first attempt to assess its value, and in its early stages it was reserved for selected criminals as a preliminary to transportation.

By the standards of the times it was successful. The aldermen of the City of London, themselves to build a new prison of their own, determined to adopt the same principle. One of the difficulties was to find an appropriate site, for within the City itself land prices were beginning to rise to an unprecedented degree. In 1842 a committee was formed to investigate the situation, eventually reporting back with details of nine different sites and schemes, either to build a new prison or to adapt an existing one. The aldermen examined each in turn, and in turn rejected them. A three-acre site in Whitecross Street, adjacent to the Debtors' Prison, would cost £142,000, while a four-acre site in Goswell Street was valued at £214,000. The cost of demolishing the Fleet Prison and enlarging the site by a further three acres was estimated at £155,000 before building started. It was therefore decided to look further afield, outside the metropolis.

One of the places considered during this new survey was a plot of land owned by the Corporation itself. It was at Holloway, immediately north of the new road connecting Holloway with Camden Town, and had been purchased by the City of London for £4,000 in 1832 as a projected burial-ground for victims of the cholera epidemic that had ravaged London the previous year. In the event the epidemic had subsided, and the land remained unused. It seemed appropriate for a new prison, for it was on high and well-drained ground, it was large enough and it was within reasonable distance of the City. Above every other consideration was the fact that the City of London already owned the site. The one slight complication was that as the land had been acquired for use as a burial-ground, it could not be used for any other purpose without an Act of Parliament. But this was obtained in 1845, and by the following year legal formalities had advanced enough to make possible the establishment of a further committee to go into the question of the cost of erecting a new prison at Holloway.

On 10 February 1848 the committee submitted its findings

to the Court of Common Council with an estimate of about £80,000, together with plans for the prison drawn up by James Bunning, architect to the City of London.

James Bunstone Bunning, born in London in 1802, had been appointed 'Clerk to the City's Works' in 1842, the twenty-first man to hold the office since it had been established in 1477. He had previously held the post of District Surveyor to Bethnal Green, in London's East End, and had been Surveyor to the estates of the Foundling Hospital. In 1840 Bunning had received a certain amount of publicity when he collaborated with I. K. Brunel in recommencing work on the Thames Tunnel at Wapping, started by Brunel's father, but abandoned for over ten years by reason of constant flooding. He had also submitted plans for the new Houses of Parliament in 1835 in a competition eventually won by Sir Charles Barry.

Bunning was therefore already well known to the aldermen of the City of London and his appointment as Clerk to the City's Works in 1842 was not entirely unexpected. The title was changed to City Architect in 1847, the year he began work on plans for the new prison at Holloway.

The official assessment of Bunning as an architect 'whose talents were more practical than artistic' (*Dictionary of National Biography*) scarcely does him justice. He was a man who shunned publicity, and it is unfortunate that some of his most interesting work, including the Metropolitan Cattle Market in Islington and the twin towers of Brunel's Hungerford Bridge at Charing Cross, have long since vanished. (It is pleasant to note the clock tower of the Metropolitan Cattle Market was restored and repaired by the GLC when the site was developed as flats and a park in 1970.) But his greatest contribution to Victorian architecture was undoubtedly his splendid London Coal Exchange of 1849, built near Billingsgate Fish Market. This circular building, constructed largely of iron and glass and topped by a dome 100ft above street level, was a landmark in architecture. In its use of cast iron and glass it was one of the

19

first and most notable examples of a technique which blossomed into such splendid fruition in Paxton's Crystal Palace in 1851 and Paddington Station a year later. Tragically, in 1962, it fell a victim to 'enlightened' planning and redevelopment and was demolished. But for this Bunning should be remembered, as he should, too, for his construction of the new Cannon Street in 1852 and his valiant efforts to preserve portions of the Roman villa unearthed on the site during excavations.

The design he submitted to the City of London in 1848 for the new House of Correction at Holloway was accepted by the aldermen, as was the estimate of cost. Early in 1849 the clearing of the site commenced, and on 26 September of that year the foundation-stone of the prison was laid by Sir James Duke, Lord Mayor of London. On it was inscribed:

May God preserve the City of London
and make this place a terror to evil-doers.

The proceedings were attended with as little publicity as possible so as not to upset local residents, and under the foundation-stone was placed a box containing coins and other Victoriana.

Bunning's brief for the new prison had been precise. It should consist of accommodation for 400 prisoners in separate cells and be capable of housing men, women and children. It must also be suitable for 'future adaptation to any mode of discipline that might hereafter be determined upon'—a clear indication that the City fathers were well aware that penal reforms were taking place and that the existing system might well be changed. The prison was to be designed on the radial principle, allowing maximum visibility and supervision by prison staff and was to include accommodation for the governor and prison chaplain.

No doubt with the grim façades of Millbank and Pentonville in mind, and in deference to the occupiers of the new and expensive villas that lined the Camden road, the prison was to be given an appearance more pleasing to the eye than that of a normal penitentiary.

The main prison block, well back from the Camden Road, consisted of a central concourse from which four blocks of cells radiated, each of four storeys. Between these and the main road stood the main entrance-gate flanked on either side by meeting-rooms, general offices and stores and a committee room for the magistrates. The façade of this group of buildings, together with the gable ends of the cell blocks, was designed in the manner of a medieval castle, supposedly that at Warwick, complete with battlements and turrets. The massive gatehouse was flanked by winged griffins representing the City of London, each bearing a key and shackles, and only a portcullis and drawbridge were lacking to complete the bizarre effect. In front of this, almost on the road, was another gatehouse, equally castellated and Tudor in appearance, while on one side stood the turretted and long-windowed residence of the governor, with the chaplain's house on the other. These two residences were accessible from the road and completed the massively-built 18ft high wall that encircled the prison.

From the centre of the prison complex rose the tall ventilation shaft, 146ft high and complete with battlements, to remain such a landmark in North London for many generations to come. This tower formed one of the first attempts at air-extraction by means of a long draught and a permanent furnace. The prison included a chapel, cookhouse, steam laundry and treadmill.

The enormous and remarkable structure demonstrated Victorian gothic in its most overpowering form, though its architectural niceties were hardly likely to be appreciated by those who went through the gates for the first time as prisoners. On 6 October 1852, quietly and with no publicity, the new prison opened its doors to receive its first inmates, 120 men and 27 women from the overcrowded penitentiary in Giltspur Street in the City. The era of Holloway had begun.

2

THE HOUSE OF CORRECTION
1852–77

The building of the City House of Correction, Holloway (as it was officially designated) was not achieved without difficulties and setbacks. There had been the problem of the site itself, and its disenfranchisement from its intended use as a burial-ground. Halfway through the construction the contractor, William Trego, had gone bankrupt, and another firm under the direction of John Jay had taken over the work, but it was finished on schedule. A few weeks before the opening date a member of the legal staff of the corporation discovered that a thirty-year-old enactment (of 1822) required that all prisons within the jurisdiction of the City should be financed by a county rate, whereas Holloway was built from corporate funds. It took a private Act of Parliament to overcome this obstacle.

The Inspector of Prisons then refused to sanction the use of the punishment cells without several alterations to the design, and on the opening day itself the Commissioner of Police for the metropolis suddenly decided he was unable to spare transport to bring prisoners from Giltspur Street gaol to the new penitentiary. As usual such problems were overcome, and the first 147 inmates were installed on the due date.

The geographical situation of the prison in fact proved less than ideal. Whilst beautifully set on rising ground with open country behind stretching north to the heights of Highgate and Hampstead, the exposed situation made access difficult in winter or bad weather. The steep incline from Islington proved too much for the heavy prison vans in such conditions, and the contractor, Arthur MacNamara, was forced to hire three-horse omnibuses to do the work, the unexpected expense apparently nearly ruining him.

When opened Holloway, with its 438 cells, provided more accommodation than any other prison administered by the City of London. It was, of course, a mixed prison, for both men and women offenders and also for boys from the age of eight upwards.

For the new arrivals the procedure was not very different from that in most prisons to this day. The prisoner was booked-in, details of age, religion and length of sentence being noted; he was weighed and examined medically, his clothes being removed, cleaned and stored against the day of his release. In many cases the clothing had to be destroyed because of its verminous condition, a situation still found today when tramps, drunks and vagrants are first taken into custody. All valuables, cash or loose possessions were removed and listed and the prisoner made to sign for them. As still happens, any jewellery or precious stones were described by their appearance only, with no assessment of their value. This precaution is intended to avoid any accusation by the prisoner on release that substitutes have been made for genuine and valuable items deposited on entry.

Prison clothes were then issued, and the prisoner interviewed by the governor or head gaoler in the reception cells before his final allocation to the appropriate block.

The cells, 13ft long, 7ft wide and 9ft high, were whitewashed and clean, each having a high, barred window at one end, and at the other a heavy door with a sliding hatch through which the warder could communicate with the inmate. Above this hatch was a small circular observation window. The cell furniture consisted of a folding table, chair, corner-cupboard and shelves, folding hammock kept on top of the cupboard during the day, wash-basin and water-closet. The books provided according to H. Mayhew and John Binny, who visited Holloway soon after its opening, included such inappropriate titles as *Life in New Zealand* and *Summer Days in the Antarctic!*

On the wall were displayed two cards, one listing the prison regulations and daily timetable, the other indicating the prisoner's name, age, offence and length of sentence. In the cell wall was a small handle which could be used to sound a gong in the corridor to attract the attention of a warder, a metal plate then showing itself above the cell door to indicate which prisoner required attention.

Each of the four cell blocks, radiating from the central concourse, were of four storeys with an open central area from roof to floor. Each storey could be distinguished by the gallery running round the perimeter with cells opening off it. Every cell on every floor was thus visible from the central area, an idea first envisaged by Jeremy Bentham in his Panopticon design for a prison at the turn of the century. The radiating wings, the arched iron roof, the galleries one above the other and the catwalks connected by spiral stairs at the central area, completed a design that was to epitomise the concept of prison for many years and for millions who would never see it in reality. It remains real to this day in such prisons as Pentonville, Wandsworth, Brixton, Bedford and countless others in many countries. In England no less than fifty-four prisons were built on this plan within fifteen years of Holloway.

Less attention had been paid to the life-style of the prisoner within the walls. The proposals made by Howard over half a century before had not penetrated most prisons. True, the classification of prisoners according to their past history, number of convictions and length of sentence was becoming normal by the time Holloway was built; but there was great disparity amongst local authorities in the treatment and punishment of offenders. Even at the 'model' prison of Pentonville, where conditions were considered so ideal that a contemporary writer was moved to ask 'What is penal about all this?', an alarming increase in insanity amongst prisoners forced the authorities to amend the regulations.

The problem was created mainly by the regime of cellular confinement, with work being brought to the cells, meals eaten alone and an insistence that prisoners should never communicate or even be able to recognise each other. They were masked when at exercise or out of their cells for any reason, a procedure described at the time as 'one of the paltriest expedients for self-deception ever invented'. Such arrangements were depressing enough to affect most prisoners adversely, but in fact it was a much smaller matter that created the most despondency. This was the glass panel in the cell door: the prisoner realised that he was never unobserved or free from supervision. This had a profound psychological effect on most prisoners, not improved by the regulation that required all warders to wear soft-soled shoes after 6pm.

As Holloway was a 'House of Correction' rather than a convict prison, conditions there were not as punitive as at Pentonville, and a modified form of separation was practised. The greater variation in the classes of prisoners, together with such amenities as classrooms, chapel and a greater amount of supervised work, made for more flexibility and a more relaxed atmosphere. Even so, though prisoners were not masked, and worked in groups in the various workrooms, officially they could not make contact or speak to each other. Work was performed in silence, and much work done outside the cell, such as oakum-picking, was carried out in high-sided booths, each prisoner being invisible to the others but all under the supervision of the warders.

The routine at Holloway a few years after it opened is described by Mayhew and Binny, in their book *Criminal Prisons of London* (1862), as follows:

6.45am—Rise, open ventilator, wash, fold bedding
7.00 to 7.30—Work
7.30 to 8.10—Breakfast, clean cell
8.10 to 9.00—Chapel service
9.00 to 12.45—Work, exercise, lessons
12.45 to 2.00—Dinner and prepare school work
2.00 to 6.45—Work, exercise, lessons
6.45 to 7.30—Work in cell and supper
7.30 to 8.00—Work in cell
8.00 to 8.45—Sweep cell, wash, read or write
8.45 to 9.00—Sling hammock and prepare for bed
9.00—Lights out

In summer the prisoners were awakened at 5.45am and performed an extra hour's work before breakfast.

With a mixed prison population aged from eight to eighty, over thirty forms of employment were in use. These included: matmaking; the treadwheel; picking oakum; general cleaning; window cleaning; whitewashing; basketmaking; bookbinding; brushmaking; assisting in infirmary; gardening; needlework; knitting; laundrywork.

All laundry for the prison was undertaken by female convicts, but no women could work in the kitchens which were manned by outside contractors, male prisoners and warders.

The treadwheel was an important part of the disciplinary system. Not only did it serve as a form of punishment, but it also had a more practical application as a source of motive power, and in Holloway was used to drive the pumps which supplied water to the prison. As far back as 1779 an Act had suggested various ways in which prisoners could be usefully employed, such as turning a capstan or a wheel to drive machinery. In 1818 a treadmill suitable for use by prisoners had been invented by William Cubitt of Lowestoft and installed in the county gaol at Bury St Edmunds.

Opinion was much divided as to the proper use of the treadmill. Many prison administrators, including several governors, looked upon it merely as a repetitious and soul-destroying form of punishment, valuable solely as a deterrent. A more enlightened attitude was adopted at Holloway, where it was seen not only as a practical form of motive power for the benefit of the prison community, but also as a means of setting the prisoners to work which they could see was useful. In some prisons outside London the work of prisoners on the treadmill was hired out to local farmers for grinding corn and similar tasks.

It was not, as is often supposed, particularly hard work. The Holloway treadmill had places for twenty-four prisoners, sixteen men and eight boys. They sat in compartments, side by side, the length of the cylinder being 54ft and its diameter 24ft. Gripping the bar in front of him each man pushed a tread downwards with his foot and pushed each tread in turn as it came into position. At Holloway twenty minutes on the tread-mill alternated with twenty minutes 'picking oakum', that standard prison occupation which consisted of unravelling old and very tough rope which later went to matmaking.

The treadmill could be dangerous, however, for as the mach-ine was activated by the combined effort of twenty-four men, if one man got into difficulties and caught a foot or leg in the machinery it was difficult to stop. At Holloway the speed was governed and accidents were rare. But in some prisons a more primitive form of machinery was used, and the men actually worked inside the wheel. At Aylesbury, as an example, the wheel installed in 1825 was removed in 1843 after three prison-ers had been crushed to death in twelve months. Yet the tread-mill continued to be an integral part of the English penal system for most of the nineteenth century, and was not officially abolished until 1898.

27

Matmaking was the most common form of employment at Holloway in the early years. The work was taught and supervised by an outside contractor, and its range was astonishing. In an age when mats were needed not only on floors but in carriages, landaus, hansoms and dog-carts there was always a steady flow of orders to the prison workshops. A particularly good customer was the London & South-Western Railway which regularly ordered mats for its carriage floors with the company initials woven into them. So successful was this project that other prisons began sending staff to Holloway for training, and by 1860 Holloway was competing with Wakefield and Preston prisons for the accolade of the prison with the highest productive capacity. Only six years later, in 1866, the thirty looms in use at Holloway had to be augmented by another thirty—a remarkable achievement.

The manufacture of clothing was another profitable venture at Holloway and the prison tailoring section supplied overcoats and other garments to other prisons in England and also to the convict colony in Gibraltar. Boys as well as men were employed in this department, and also in the shoemaking shop; so at least some of the convicts had an opportunity of learning a trade which, it was hoped, would result in their leading a more industrious life after release.

Bearing in mind the attitude of the authorities to prisoners only a century before, it is interesting to note the concern which the staff at Holloway displayed for the future welfare of those under their charge.

A vital part of this rehabilitation, which began immediately on entering Holloway, was the range of classes provided daily. Mayhew's account of Holloway, written in 1862, includes an interview with the head teacher of the day, a Mr Barre, who seems to have been an enthusiastic and enlightened man. The great majority of prisoners needed instruction in reading and writing, and this they did on slates, for no copybooks were provided. The young prisoners were particularly interested in

28

reading, at which, says Barre, they showed far greater aptitude than did the older inmates. The adults, on the whole, were more proficient at arithmetic, a not surprising conclusion in view of the fact that many were serving sentences for fraud and false pretences. Additional subjects taught were history and geography, together with 'the elements of general knowledge'. Singing classes were conducted weekly, based on Hullah's System of Music, though these were restricted to the best-behaved inmates.

Barre obviously took his work extremely seriously and was convinced that the more his pupils learned in prison the less likely they were to return. He actively encouraged his brighter pupils, and was not averse to continuing private tuition in their cells. 'I find that if they feel that people are really interested in them there is less likelihood of their misconducting themselves' was his comment.

Female prisoners in Holloway had their own woman teacher, but numbers were of course smaller. On the other hand the women seemed, on the whole, better at reading and writing than the men, and were particularly interested in geography.

No prisoner of either sex whose sentence was less than six weeks was allowed to attend classes. For those who could use it a circulating library was available, each convict being allowed to choose two books a week. They were all of 'a moral and religious character'. Well-educated prisoners, of whom there were many men but virtually no women, did not have to attend classes but spent the appropriate session writing a précis of that morning's sermon.

All prisoners were expected to attend chapel daily, the building being large enough to accommodate the entire prison population including staff. At Holloway the inmates sat in pews, unlike the system at Wandsworth and Pentonville where each sat in a high-sided, gated box, invisible to others. The chaplain, governor and any visiting magistrates sat on either side of the pulpit facing the prisoners, while warders sat amongst the inmates in the body of the chapel and in the gallery, which communicated direct with the upper storeys of the cell-blocks. Mayhew, who attended various services at Holloway, remarks on the variety of faces and expression seen amongst the prisoners and was obviously surprised to find several 'of respectable appearance and with an engaging manner . . . indicating an acute and lively mind'. There were others, however, whom he conjectured, because of their arched eyebrows and peculiar features, 'were of Hibernian extraction'. All sects attended chapel, the only exception being, on this occasion, 'one Roman Catholic, a very eccentric man'.

The duties of the chaplain at Holloway were rather more extensive than might be expected. His main function was to minister to the spiritual welfare of prisoners through sermons and also by requiring them to commit to memory selected texts 'suitable to their position and state of mind'. He worked in close liaison with the British Ladies' Society for Promoting the Reformation of Female Prisoners, an organisation which stemmed from Elizabeth Fry's earlier experiments at Newgate. But also, rather in the guise of under-cover agent, he talked to all prisoners in turn and, on the pretext of religious and reformative discussion, attempted to elicit from them information on previous convictions, outside associations, family details, and other facts on general conditions of life and work, that were recorded and passed on to the prison authorities. Not all chaplains were happy about this aspect of their work, and there is evidence that some refused to question prisoners on anything but their religious background and beliefs. But Holloway's first chaplain, the Rev James Cohen, who remained until 1860, was most enthusiastic and, working closely with Barre, the head teacher, was able to supply a fund of information on prisoners and their background which was of undoubted value to the Government inspectors and the few social workers of the time.

The Rev John Owen, who was chaplain at the time of Mayhew's visits, says little about this side of his work, but expands on how his religious teaching in prison has opened the eyes of many inmates to the existence of God and persuaded them to mend their ways. 'The solitude of the cell has a beneficial effect on most characters not hardened by vice.'

Whatever the benefits claimed, there is little evidence that the cellular system engendered much spirit of penitence or zeal for reform in those who suffered it.

During its first twenty-five years of existence under the jurisdiction of the City of London, Holloway was used to capacity. The number of inmates averaged 400, consisting of about 300 men, 75 women and 25 juveniles. On a par with Pentonville, but less than half the size of Millbank or Wandsworth, Holloway was still the largest penitentiary administered by the City. Millbank was a Government convict prison while Wandsworth, together with the first all-female prison at Brixton, was under the control of the county of Surrey. The Aldermen of the City of London, therefore, were much concerned that the prison staff should be adequate in number and efficient in their duties. The record for the first few years indicates that their objective was not entirely achieved. In 1855, three years after opening, the establishment of Holloway was as follows:

> Governor
> Chaplain
> Resident surgeon
> Chief warder
> Principal warder
> 8 Warders
> 6 Assistant warders
> 1 Matron
> 3 Female warders
> 1 Schoolmaster

1 Schoolmistress
1 Storeman
1 Clerk to the governor
1 Porter
1 Cook
1 Engineer
1 Messenger
1 General labourer

thus providing a ratio of 1 warder to twenty prisoners.

The governor appointed on opening was George Wright, an ex-lieutenant of the Royal Navy and deputy governor of Newgate. Wright, whose starting salary was £400 a year plus free living accommodation, was a keen and conscientious man who, during his first two years in office, refused to take a holiday. In 1858 his salary was increased to £550 by the City Aldermen, who expressed their satisfaction in the way he had performed his duties and presented him with a gratuity of 100 guineas as a mark of their esteem. Their satisfaction was short-lived. Little more than a year later, in March 1859, the City auditors, unable to obtain certain financial information from the governor, decided to examine the accounts more closely. A deficiency of £200 was revealed in Wright's figures, which he was unable to explain. At length the truth came out. It was a sorry tale, and one all too common. Wright had unwisely guaranteed the business venture of a friend, which had failed and so rendered him liable for the debts. In addition his wife had fallen ill and had been bedridden for two years, while the final blow was the death of three of his four children within twelve months. There was virtually no chance of repayment.

Though his conduct could not be overlooked, Wright had been a popular and efficient governor and there were many to speak in his favour. The Aldermen exercised mercy and did not press charges. He was quietly dismissed later that year and vanished from the scene. His successor in 1859 was John

Page 33 (above) General view of Holloway Prison, 1865; *(below)* prisoners picking oakum, 1862; note the men in numbered booths working a treadmill

Page 34 (left) The Black Maria leaving Bow Street, 1887; (*below*) W. T. Stead (1849–1912) the famous editor of the *Pall Mall Gazette,* about 1900

Weatherhead, also from Newgate, who was destined to hold the post for the next twenty years.

Nor, in those early days, were the Aldermen free of troubles with the prison staff. There was friction between male and female warders, and an official memo comments sorrowfully that 'There has not been that cordiality which ought to have existed on the female side.' Excess cordiality, however, proved the downfall of Sarah Marchant, one of the first female warders, who was dismissed after arriving at the prison in a riotously intoxicated state. A similar fate befell the driver of the prison van bringing the prisoners from Bow Street and other London courts; on one occasion he was so drunk that he had to be put inside the 'Black Maria', while an obliging 'client' drove it from the City to Holloway. He was an employee of the contractor, MacNamara, and was immediately replaced by a driver employed by the corporation.

The first schoolmaster soon had to be dismissed for incompetence, and the first medical officer of Holloway, Gilbert MacMurdo, who already attended at Giltspur Street and Newgate, was obviously too old to undertake the extra work and was tactfully removed. He was replaced by Thomas Graham, a much younger man, who was appointed at a salary of £150 a year in 1854, with £50 for the supply of medicines. He was also required to live within a quarter-mile of the prison. Though agreeing to the conditions of employment Graham began to object very soon to his duties, in particular to the necessity of visiting warders who were off sick in their homes. In addition he insisted that the £50 allowance was only for medication supplied to prisoners and did not cover the needs of staff. Things came to a head when Graham made a lengthy journey to visit a warder who was supposedly ill, only to find that he was out shopping and, in any case, was returning to work next day. The doctor complained to the governor and the matter came before a special meeting of the gaol committee. In the event the committee backed the governor, rebuking the young doctor for being 'difficult' and making the enquiry necessary. At the same time it expressed its satisfaction in his general work by presenting him with a brand new case of surgical instruments!

John Weatherhead, the governor, was still concerned with expenditure on drugs and in 1871 removed the onus of their purchase from Dr Graham, making a deal with the Society of Apothecaries to provide all medicaments for the prisoners' needs for £25 a year.

By this time debtors were being housed in Holloway. Their demands were more exacting than those of ordinary felons, and they were allowed more privileges. As compensation for the extra work, Graham was given an increase in salary of £30 in 1873. He remained medical officer to the prison for over twenty years, but in 1877, when Holloway came under the jurisdiction of the Home Office, moved away from the prison to Finsbury Park, appointed a deputy and exercised his function mainly in a supervisory capacity.

While complaints and representations about working conditions were treated with some sympathy when coming from the medical staff, chaplain or teachers, this did not apply to the prison staff as a whole. Warders were appointed between the ages of twenty-one and thirty-five, with preference being given to officers of the Metropolitan police. The rules of conduct were rigorous and applied not only to their duties in the prison but to their private lives as well. Any warder thought to be in any way affected by alcohol, either in the prison or at home, was liable to instant dismissal, and there were strict warnings about frequenting public houses when off duty. Smoking anywhere on the prison premises was strictly forbidden, even during rest-periods. The hours were long, normally thirteen to fifteen hours daily with only one Sunday off in seven. In 1865 the prison was visited by magistrates under the new scheme of inspection, and as a result of their report hours were reduced to a maximum of twelve daily and free Sundays

increased to one in three. These benefits, however, were somewhat negatived by the City Aldermen when they refused to
engage more staff to cover the reduced hours on the curious
pretext that the warders' duties were now much lighter!

Compared with the hours worked by some other prison
personnel the warders were not ill-used. Worst off were the
night-watchmen who, until 1873, were on duty every night of
the year except Christmas night. Pay, too, at Holloway was
lower than at other prisons in London for the first few years,
though after 1860 a system of annual increments was adopted.
These were not automatic, but had to be petitioned for to the
governor, who had power to refuse if he considered them
undeserved. But by 1872 Holloway had come into line with other
prisons and a general and automatic annual increment of
10 per cent inaugurated.

Over the years since 1853 the duties of the prison staff had
certainly become more onerous, not because of the increase in
prisoners (for the prison was always full) but because of a
change in the type of inmate. The biggest upset was in 1870
when the abolition of the Debtors' Prison brought its residents
to Holloway. These, of course, were civil prisoners as distinct
from criminals and of a type not previously handled in the
prison. They could claim special dietary regimes, were allowed
to smoke and had privileges that were totally outside the
normal routine of Holloway. Further trouble was created by
the unwillingness of the county-court bailiffs to accept that
prisoners could not be admitted to Holloway after 10pm, and a
major furore was caused when one bailiff attempted to deliver
a highly-intoxicated and musically-inclined debtor at one in
the morning.

For the general run of felons in the prison such incidents
must have been a welcome relief from the grinding and overpowering boredom of life. Confined to their cells when not
working, at chapel or at school, when at exercise each prisoner
had to keep at least three yards away from his nearest com-

37

panion, to walk with hands clasped behind his back and to look straight ahead, not forgetting to salute the chief warder if he should appear. Needless to say, silence was maintained at all times. Yet discipline was good and there was little unrest. The general state of health was also good, considering the primitive rules of hygiene. Typhus, typhoid and the dreaded smallpox were frequent visitors to the metropolis in the 1850s and 1860s, yet apart from one death from typhoid in the summer of 1857 Holloway had no fatalities from these scourges and remarkably few deaths of any kind. It is, therefore, not surprising that despite the routine allowing a hot bath just once a fortnight in summer and only once a month in winter, and forbidding the cutting of female prisoners' hair, Holloway's record in health matters, as in discipline, was looked upon as a model, and its rules were copied by several newly opened prisons.

Whilst the general standard of conduct of the inmates was satisfactory, one or two unfortunate instances emerge from the reports. Selina Salter, for instance, a twenty-three-year-old Irish girl sentenced to prison in 1857, managed during her time in Holloway to destroy the furniture in 13 cells, tear up 6 prison gowns and all her clothing, and be reported 400 times for refusing labour and 200 times for violent and outrageous conduct. She was returned to her father on six occasions and, in desperation, sent to America twice, but each time she reappeared at Holloway on further charges. Detailed reports of Selina's conduct indicate that all this was unusual even for the most spirited prisoners! But she has some marginal interest in that her behaviour, and that of other prisoners or defendants obviously suffering from acute mental disturbance, led to the Criminal Lunatics Act of 1860, and the establishment of Britain's first criminal lunatic asylum at Broadmoor in 1863. Broadmoor's architect, incidentally, was the same Major-General (now Sir) Joshua Jebb who had designed the 'Model Prison' at Pentonvelle twenty years before; at Broadmoor he devised a completely different layout, but as can still be seen, it looks much more like a prison than the hospital it really is. Security was of course uppermost in the minds of all prison administrators at the time.

In the same year that Broadmoor was opened the governor of Holloway introduced more stringent security arrangements, which included the iron-plating of the cell doors on the inner side. A Home Office circular on the subject of prison security issued in 1867 resulted in the augmenting of the prison armoury to include seventeen pistols or revolvers, twenty-four rifles and seventeen cutlasses. For a short time armed guards were required to accompany the prisoners travelling from the courts to prison, but as far as Holloway was concerned this was soon abandoned.

In its work as a House of Correction, in its health record, in its workshops' output and in its humane handling of comparatively short-term prisoners, Holloway was more of a 'model' penitentiary than was Pentonville. The City of London was proud of it. It was therefore with something of a shock that the City Aldermen learned that the Act of 1865, which had attempted to impose some sort of uniformity in the handling of prisoners in local prisons, had not been altogether successful, and few had achieved such standards as Holloway. The implications were becoming obvious. If local prisons could not, or would not, comply with the recommendations of the Home Office, then the Home Office must take over responsibility for all penal establishments in Britain.

Admittedly, the problems of the administrators of local prisons had been caused more by shortage of finance than by any unwillingness to comply with the standards. The solution had to be the removal of all prisons from the jurisdiction of the local authorities. By the Prisons Act of 1877, they were placed directly under the control of the Home Office. This measure fundamentally affected the basis of local government, and was to have a profound effect on the British penal system.

3
HOLLOWAY UNDER THE HOME OFFICE

The Prisons Act of 1877, in transferring to the central government the responsibility for all local prisons, had not been accepted by Parliament without opposition. At the second reading of the Bill in 1876 it had been denounced as 'a distinct slur on local management' and as 'sapping the foundations . . . of independent local administration'. But it was inevitable that the Bill would become law, and much preparation had gone on during its passage through Parliament to ensure that immediate action could be taken once this was achieved.

The Act became operative on 1 April 1878, and on that very day no less than 38 of the 112 local prisons passing to the Home Office were closed, with 19 others closing during the next ten years. The local authorities themselves viewed the process with mixed feelings, though whatever doubts they may have had about the new system and its effects were allayed by consideration of the financial burden from which they would be relieved.

The City of London did not welcome the innovation, for in Holloway they had a prison in which standards were already high and where the financial burden was comparatively light.

The transfer affected the staff of the prison, who became civil servants under the jurisdiction of the Home Office, leaving the employment of the Corporation of the City of London. On the transfer the City Aldermen, showing a surprising humanity, handed out gratuities to their ex-employees ranging from 100 guineas to the governor down to two weeks' pay for the most menial members of the staff. Even more remarkable was the fact that for the next forty years the Aldermen of the City met annually to administer pensions and look into questions of hardship resulting from the change. It was not until 1917 that the last payment was made, on the death of an ex-warder, thus finally bringing to an end the City of London's official association with Holloway Prison.

As indicated by the immediate closure of so many prisons, the Home Office intended to unify the prison system with the greatest possible speed. This was to be undertaken by a panel of Prison Commissioners not exceeding five in number, of which the first chairman was Sir Edward du Cane, a military man, and Sir Joshua Jebb's successor as Director-General of Convict Prisons. For the first time both convict and local prisons now came under one authority; the Prison Commissioners were directly responsible to the Home Secretary. In view of what was to come there was little chance that du Cane, an unimaginative military martinet, would be forgotten in a hurry (even if his name had not been perpetuated in a road near Wormwood Scrubs Prison!).

Arrangements went ahead to transfer from Holloway the assets belonging to the Corporation, including the revenue from goods made by prisoners, while the prison itself and the land on which it stood was conveyed to the new Prison Commissioners. Here trouble arose, for part of the land acquired by the City over forty years before had never been used as part of the prison premises. Accordingly the City Corporation insisted that they should be allowed to retain it, or, alternatively, that it should be bought by the Home Office at a price taking

41

into account how greatly the value had increased since the original purchase. They also pointed out, with truth, that the land involved had never been considered or bought as part of a prison scheme, as it had orginally been intended for a cemetery.

The argument raged loud and long, and as might be imagined, the government had its way, but the victory was not complete, for the Home Office contented itself by making a compulsory purchase of a twenty-foot strip of land round the perimeter of the prison, for security reasons, leaving the remainder, now virtually useless, to the City. This action, incidentally, was carried out despite protestations from the City's lawyers claiming that it was illegal.

The main object of the new Prison Commission under du Cane was the standardisation of prison administration throughout the country. Such matters as working conditions for staff, the keeping of accounts and the system of local purchase of food and other requirements had varied widely from one authority to another. Now new regulations were to ensure that the same system applied in all prisons. Even an Inspector of Medical Services was appointed, so that similar standards of health and hygiene for both inmates and staff could be applied.

It was less simple to devise an all-pervading system for the treatment of prisoners. In theory any such system should take into account the social background of the prisoner, his previous criminal history and his type of offence. In practice, although some of these factors were taken into consideration, such as the segregation of debtors from criminals and their dispensation from wearing prison clothes, the regime that du Cane imposed was brought to bear on all types of prisoners in the interest of efficient administration.

One of the first results of the new thinking was the introduction of what was termed the Progressive Stage System. This allowed prisoners to earn money by means of a system of marks once they had served the initial stage of 28 days' imprisonment. Four stages of progress through prison were defined, with an easing of the type and hours of work, better sleeping arrangements and other privileges being allowed as the inmate progressed from one to another. Any misdemeanour or transgression of prison rules meant a loss of marks which, in effect, could mean extra time spent in one stage or even relegation to a lower stage. Some of the conditions applying at each stage were as follows:

Stage 1. Ten hours' hard labour daily, of which 6 hours minimum to be spent at the treadwheel or crank. Bed to be a plank with no mattress. Up to 8 marks awarded daily, but no cash to be earned. On the collection of 224 marks transfer to

Stage 2. Duties to be second-class (general prison duties but no hard labour). A mattress allowed on a plank for five nights out of seven. Attendance at prison school allowed and schoolbooks allowed in cell. Exercise allowed on Sundays. Cash earnings on the basis of one penny for every 20 marks, with a maximum of one shilling.

Stage 3. As above, but with a mattress allowed six nights out of seven, library books allowed in cell, and earnings up to 1s 6d.

Stage 4. Prisoner could be employed in a position of trust. A mattress allowed every night. Permission to send and receive one letter every 3 months and to receive a visitor for 20 minutes every 3 months. Maximum earnings increased to 2s.

The system was to continue virtually unchanged for the next twenty years. At Holloway, however, the high incidence of short-term prisoners serving correctional training made it unlikely that many would ever reach Stages 3 and 4. The result was a situation that persists in many prisons to this day—the minor and therefore short-term offender is treated more harshly and allowed fewer privileges than the more dangerous criminal serving a long sentence.

The effect of the du Cane administration was to engender administrative efficiency, but to take no account of prisoners as individuals. Individuality was stifled and the brutalising began. Prisoners began their sentences as human beings, but

43

too often emerged sullen, suspicious and even more resentful of authority, and frequently suffering from tuberculosis and deficiency diseases which made them virtually unemployable. In this condition their only recourse was to return to crime.

Not that du Cane was particularly concerned with the end-product of his prison system. As a high-ranking civil servant he was more concerned with statistics, and in 1881, after four years of his regime, was able to report the following examples of how efficient his system had proved:

1. The total number of prisons in England and Wales had been reduced from 113 to 67, though the prison population had declined only marginally (from 27,392 in 1877 to 26,220 in 1881).

2. There had been large reductions in prison staff.

3. Special provisions for Roman Catholic prisoners now applied.

4. There was uniform treatment and discipline in all prisons.

5. Improvement in diet had been achieved, as well as betterment of hygiene.

6. There had been a reduction in the annual death-rate in prison from 10.8 per thousand in 1877 to 8.73 per thousand in 1881.

7. The annual number of suicides in prison had also fallen— from 18 to 14 in the same period.

8. The need for the more stringent forms of punishment had been reduced. Floggings had dropped from an annual average of 11 to 9, and the number of prisoners on 'bread and water' diet had been almost halved.

9. The annual government grant to assist discharged prisoners had increased from under £3,000 to over £6,000.

An important innovation, in 1879, had been the introduction of the 'Star' class for first offenders. This was intended to be a means of identifying and segregating the newcomers from the 'old lags', but it created problems (as it still does) when convicted murderers were given 'Star' class on the grounds that they had never previously served a prison sentence.

The du Cane regime, whilst applauded by those who had put it into practice, was by no means the success it claimed to be when judged in terms of humane treatment and the correction of criminal ways. The proportion of recidivists continued to rise, which was in direct contrast to the expressed hopes of du Cane himself: whilst admitting the degrading and brutalising effect of his system, he maintained that it was the only means of creating an effective deterrent for criminals.

So the regime's results, as distinct from its administrative efficiency, caused growing concern amongst informed people. The savagery and inhumanity of the English penal system became notorious abroad, and received criticism even from such an unlikely quarter as the prison authorities in Tsarist Russia! At home, criticism came mainly from the more thinking prison officers, though then, as now, they were debarred by the Home Office from publicising their opinions. Amongst those who felt particularly strongly on the subject was a prison chaplain, the Rev W. Morrison, who in defiance of the censorship imposed by the Home Office, wrote a series of articles in the press revealing the cruelties of the system and castigating du Cane and the Prison Commissioners. Though relieved of his post as a prison chaplain, Morrison continued to expose the system, and was encouraged and supported by the national press.

Public opinion eventually became so outspoken that in 1894 the Liberal government of the day set up a special committee to report on conditions in prisons. The committee, in its preliminary report, decided there was 'ample cause for a searching enquiry into prison life', and this was immediately begun. Fortunately du Cane himself was on the point of retiring, and tactfully did so without the embarrassment of featuring personally in the findings that followed. He was replaced that same year by Sir Evelyn Ruggles-Brise, a man of more enlightened and flexible mentality who was destined to make some of the most far-reaching improvements in the prison system since the recommendations of John Howard a century before.

It was against this background of rigorous prison discipline and ruthless drive for efficiency, with a minority but steadily-growing demand for more humanity in the treatment of prisoners, that Holloway continued as a mixed prison for the final quarter of the nineteenth century. Throughout its history, and largely due to the enlightened attitude of the Corporation of the City of London, Holloway had had a name for combining efficiency with treatment far more humane than was customary in similar penitentiaries elsewhere. Even before the Home Office had taken over in 1877, a system of payments had been inaugurated in the prison, and as early as 1860 a scale of fines evolved not only for unruly prisoners, but for lax prison officers. These included a fine of 1s for failure to lock a prisoner's cell, a similar amount for 'wrangling on duty', 6d for failure to provide a prisoner with paper to write on, and 6d for falling asleep in chapel! Other fines were imposed for any officer entering a prisoner's cell at night unaccompanied, and the regulations also insisted that not only should prison officers not 'wrangle' but, despite their secret feelings, must at all times present 'a calm demeanour'.

As a mixed prison, and also as a remand prison for those arrested and waiting trial, Holloway at various times housed both the famous and the infamous. As a 'local prison' under the City of London it had not, like Pentonville, been used as a convict prison for those whose fate was penal servitude overseas. The local prisons (the title of 'House of Correction' had been abolished in 1865) were subject to certain regulations applicable only to short-term prisoners. One of these was the classification of prisoners into two divisions according to the type of offence. Prisoners convicted of misdemeanours which did not attract the performance of hard labour were allocated to the First Division and, though deprived of their freedom, were spared the more rigorous and unpleasant aspects of the fate allotted to true 'criminals'. First Division prisoners were often those sentenced for contempt of court, seditious libel and orders imposed by the courts for so-called 'non-criminal' offences. Those whose transgressions were of a more serious nature were allocated to the Second Division with the privations and hardships that it incurred. An even stricter Third Division was inaugurated later. Holloway received a high proportion of Second Division prisoners. It was now very crowded, for by 1885 the total number of prisons in England had been further reduced to 59.

It was in that year that the Criminal Law Amendment Act came into force, the curious result of which was the arrest, trial and subsequent imprisonment in Holloway of the man who had worked hardest to make it law—the newspaper editor W. T. Stead. (Ten years later it was to result in the imprisonment in Holloway of an even more flamboyant character—Oscar Wilde.)

Stead was greatly concerned with the lot of the poor and ill-educated in London, and through the medium of his paper —the *Pall Mall Gazette*—conducted vigorous campaigns for the improvement of conditions and the righting of the many injustices he saw around him. One of the worst scandals of the time was the thriving trade in child prostitutes. This was created by an anomaly in the law which declared that thirteen was a girl's age of consent for sexual intercourse. This meant that on her thirteenth birthday cruel and unscrupulous parents in the East End of London could sell their child to a brothel-keeper on the grounds that the girl was of the age of consent and knew what she was doing. The anomaly appeared in the fact that elsewhere it was decreed that a child of thirteen years was too young to appreciate the significance of the oath in a court-of-law, and could therefore not be subpoenaed as a witness! Both parents and brothel-keepers were protected by these two opposing decisions, and the vicious trade flourished.

In 1881 Lord Shaftesbury and others had tried to introduce a Bill after a Commission of Enquiry had confirmed the existence of this trade, but as neither political party saw much capital in it the matter was not actively pursued.

Stead determined to negotiate the purchase of a girl himself, apparently sell her to a brothel, and expose the situation in a series of articles in his paper. The assistance of a former brothel-keeper was enlisted, and a young girl of thirteen, Eliza Armstrong, was bought from her mother and taken to a brothel. She was locked in an upstairs room, medically examined and pronounced a virgin, visited by Stead and then whisked away to Paris in the care of the Salvation Army before any harm could befall her.

Stead had his evidence, and the articles which followed, under the title 'The Maiden Tribute of Modern Babylon', describing exactly how the purchase and sale was effected, caused a scandal of unprecedented proportions. But unfortunately for Stead things went wrong. Firstly Mrs Armstrong, on reading of the affair involving her daughter, denied that she had sold the child for immoral purposes and insisted that she was told she would be going into domestic service. Secondly Stead was under the impression Mrs Armstrong was a widow. She was not, and an irate Mr Armstrong then appeared and complained that his permission had not been sought.

The final chain in this unfortunate series of events was that when the Armstrongs wrote to the Salvation Army in Paris demanding the return of their daughter, the letter went astray and Eliza was not returned. The parents accordingly went to the police, and the luckless Stead was arrested and charged with abduction. In the meantime the affair had caused such an outcry that the government had no option but hurriedly to pass the Bill, and the Criminal Law Amendment Act came into force claiming Stead as its first victim.

The case created a world-wide sensation. Many of Stead's friends were convinced the trial would be a mere formality, but Stead, by now more conversant with the law and realising he had no defence, was not so sanguine. He forecast a sentence of three months, and despite a fighting fund of £6,000 and witnesses for the defence who included the Archbishop of Canterbury, Cardinal Manning and Mr Balfour, he was found guilty. His forecast was correct. He was sentenced to three months' imprisonment, to count from the day of his arrest, leaving two months to be served in custody. Stead was taken first to the prison at Coldbath Fields, where he was treated as a criminal, his hair cropped, made to wear prison uniform and subjected to the normal procedure meted out to a Second Division convict. Three days later he was suddenly removed from Coldbath and transferred to Holloway, upgraded to First Division and given privileges even greater than was customary in that enlightened establishment.

Stead's own account of his two months in Holloway is almost ecstatic. 'Never had I a pleasanter holiday, a more charming season of repose,' he writes. 'Here as in an enchanted castle, jealously guarded by liveried retainers, I was kept secure from the strife of tongues and afforded the rare luxury of journalistic leisure.' It is doubtful if many of Holloway's 400 inmates looked on their confinement in quite that light! The truth was that Stead was not being treated like a prisoner at all. In his cell on E Wing he had papers, books, flowers and 'everything that heart could wish'.

One of the provisions covering First Division prisoners was that, where possible, they should be allowed to work at their own trade. Stead's trade was journalism, and the staff of the *Pall Mall Gazette* visited him each morning at Holloway to receive instructions and to take down copy for leaders and articles which he wrote. Stead was highly amused at comments in some periodicals which deplored the 'erratic course the *Gazette* was taking in the absence of the editor's guiding hand'. The erratic articles complained of, he pointed out, were usually from his own pen and written in his cell.

49

Visitors were allowed daily, the only exception being those who had been intimately concerned with him in the matters leading to his conviction. Even so, they all had to be listed and previously approved by the prison authorities, and even the great Cecil Rhodes, on a visit to England in December 1885 and wishing to congratulate Stead personally, was barred from seeing him when he arrived at Holloway unannounced.

Stead's wife visited him twice weekly, and declared somewhat wryly that she was now seeing more of him than she had done since the whole affair started six months before. His food was sent over from the nearby Holloway Castle Tavern and he had his own gas-ring and kettle. Like all other prisoners he was required to attend chapel daily ('the best-attended place of worship in North London' as a warder put it), sitting in the chief warder's pew from where he faced his fellow prisoners and could observe them. His comments on their appearance are entertaining. 'The prisoners in appearance are as respectable-looking as members of Parliament. Some of course are worse, but many are better.'

He became friendly with the chaplain at Holloway, Mr Plaford, though he thought his attitude to the prisoners somewhat unfair, particularly at Christmas, when he told Stead that anyone in gaol at that time of year must be there because he had trampled underfoot any love and affection he may once have had for his family. 'The good chaplain,' said Stead, 'would do better if he were to read once in a way not merely the Gospel according to St Matthew but the Gospel according to Victor Hugo in *Les Miserables*!' Though he had been supported in his campaign by the highest church dignitaries in the land, Stead seems to have been unfortunate with the prison chaplains he encountered. During his first three days of punitive imprisonment in Coldbath Fields he was to say later that the only person who treated him with rudeness and had not one kind word to say to him was the chaplain.

Christmas 1885 was celebrated in Holloway by Stead in

Page 51 (*above*) Prisoners at exercise, 1890; (*below*) meeting discharged prisoners outside the gates, 1890

Page 52 (*right*) Inside a cell in 1947—only slight improvements over the 1909 arrangements; (*below*) a magazine illustration showing 'The Scene of the Suffragettes' Martyrdom in Holloway Prison'; the top two pictures show the day and night arrangements of normal cells and the bottom two show the arrangements for consumptives (larger windows)

traditional manner, surrounded by his family and friends, and he even had a special New Year card printed, decorated with his portrait and a drawing of the famous entrance. On 18 January 1886, Stead was released, and once again directed the *Pall Mall Gazette* from his own office, where he continued his crusades against bureaucracy and inequality as vigorously as before. But never again did he undertake such a dangerous experiment, though his own self-confidence was never in doubt. Of his period in Holloway he later wrote: 'As I was taking my exercise in the prison yard this morning I asked myself who was the man of most importance alive. I could find only one answer—the prisoner in this cell.' His long and colourful career came to a tragic end in 1912 when he was lost in the *Titanic*.

Three years after Stead's term in Holloway there came up for trial at the Old Bailey one of the most amazing women swindlers of all time. This was Mrs Gordon-Baillie, a name which was one of the forty-one aliases used by Scottish-born Mary Anderson during her seventeen-year career of international fraud and false pretences. In England she claimed to be the daughter of a Scottish laird and wealthy land-owner and for some years financed herself by appeals to public figures for money to ease the terrible plight of the Scottish crofters which was causing concern in 1884 and 1885. She was of handsome and striking appearance, well spoken and impeccably dressed in clothes mostly obtained, with cheques subsequently dishonoured, from stores up and down the country.

Many well-known figures fell for her charms, including Stead himself, who published an impassioned appeal in the *Pall Mall Gazette* urging his readers to subscribe to the Gordon-Baillie fund for poor crofters. Soon after this the good lady vanished from the scene to reappear in Canada, then America and eventually in Australia, with visits to England under various assumed names in between. Her career of international fraud came to an end in 1888 when the police finally caught-up with her and she was charged at Bow Street. Her next few weeks were spent in Holloway until her trial at the Old Bailey, where she was sentenced to five years penal servitude, the major part of which she spent in Holloway until she was removed to Woking, to which all female convicts in the London area were transferred in 1892.

Notorious as Mrs Gordon-Baillie became during her trial, the most colourful and famous figure to be lodged in Holloway while it was still a mixed prison was undoubtedly Oscar Wilde. The account of Wilde and his liaison with Lord Alfred Douglas has been the subject of innumerable books, some reliable and others most certainly not. It will therefore be sufficient to recall that as a result of the evidence available in defence of Lord Queensberry's allegations of Wilde's immoral behaviour, in respect of which Wilde unwisely sued him for libel in March 1895, Wilde was advised to withdraw the charge halfway through the case and Queensberry was acquitted. It was therefore inevitable that Wilde himself would be charged with immoral behaviour under that same Act of 1885 which Stead had worked so valiantly to get through Parliament ten years earlier. Accordingly Wilde was arrested a few days later (after refusing to flee abroad as his friends strongly advised) and was charged at Bow Street on 6 April. The case was adjourned for a week, the judge refusing bail, and Wilde was remanded in custody to Holloway. There he remained up to and throughout his first trial, which began on 26 April, until released on bail a fortnight before his second trial and subsequent conviction on 25 May.

Between his arrest and release on bail five weeks later Wilde was at first visited daily in Holloway by Lord Alfred Douglas —the 'Bosie' who had contributed so greatly to his downfall. The day before the trial began Douglas was persuaded to go to France, much against his will: if the verdict went against Wilde, as seemed likely, Bosie himself would almost certainly be arrested and charged with a similar offence. Indeed, such was the degree of public feeling at the time that the foreman of the jury went as far as to enquire whether a warrant had yet been issued for the arrest of Douglas. In the event the jury disagreed at the end of the trial on 1 May, and a second trial was arranged for 20 May. On 7 May Wilde was released from Holloway on bail of £5,000. No hotel in London would risk accommodating him, and after a brief stay with his mother in Chelsea, he was put up by his good friends Ada and Ernest Leverson. At his second trial, which ended on 25 May, Wilde was found guilty and sentenced to two years' hard labour. The first six months were spent in Pentonville and Wandsworth, the remaining eighteen months in Reading, the gaol with which Wilde will always be most closely associated.

Though Wilde was in Holloway for only five weeks it was his first experience of prison life and deprivation of liberty, and as such was a profound shock and humiliation to a man who, almost more than any other living person, embodied the 'bohemianism' of his day. 'Bosie' Douglas came to visit him daily and Wilde's letters to the Leversons, More Adey, Robert Ross and other friends indicate how much he looked forward to these visits. On 9 April he wrote to Ada Leverson: 'Not that I am really alone. A slim thing, gold-haired like an angel, stands always by my side. He moves in the gloom like a wild flower.' In fact Bosie's visits to Holloway must have been anything but comfortable, according to his own account. In his autobiography he writes:

> I used to see Oscar every day at Holloway in that ghastly way that 'visits' are arranged in prisons. The visitor goes into a box rather like the box in a pawnshop. There is a whole row of these boxes, each occupied by a visitor, and opposite, facing each visitor, is the prisoner whom he is visiting. The two sides of visitors and prisoners are separated by a corridor about a yard in width, and a warder paces up and down the corridor. The 'visit' lasts, as far as I can remember, a quarter of an hour. The visitor and the prisoner have to shout to make their voices heard above the voices of other prisoners and visitors. Nothing

more revolting and cruel and deliberately malignant could be devised by human ingenuity. And it is to be remembered that I am speaking of a remand prison, where the prisoners are awaiting trial, and possibly quite innocent of any offence whatsoever. Poor Oscar was rather deaf. He could hardly hear what I said in the babel. He looked at me with tears running down his cheeks and I looked at him. Such as it was, as he told me in nearly every letter (and he wrote every day with clockwork regularity) this interview was the only bright spot in the day. He looked forward to it with pathetic eagerness. There was literally nothing else I could do for him. The world outside the prison, as represented by the newspapers, was howling for his blood like a pack of wolves.

Less than a year after the Wilde scandal Holloway received another famous prisoner in the person of Dr Jameson, 'hero' of the Jameson Raid and friend and confidante of Cecil Rhodes. Jameson frequently acted as a go-between for Rhodes in his dealing with various native tribal leaders, notably Lobengula, chief of the Matabele. Towards the end of 1895 Jameson attempted to cross the Transvaal to help the Uitlanders in Johannesburg and, proceeding without the knowledge or consent of Rhodes, rode into an ambush and was captured by the Boer general Cronje in January 1896. He was released by Kruger only on condition that he was sent back to England and tried under the Foreign Enlistment Act. Rhodes was forced to resign the premiership of Cape Colony and Jameson came home and was duly tried and sentenced to eighteen months in the First Division, which he served in Holloway. He later returned to South Africa and was himself appointed premier of Cape Colony in 1904. He died in 1917.

While Holloway was the temporary residence of a few such famous figures, more than a few people were concerned not only with the conditions of the 400 or so ordinary prisoners that made up the day-to-day complement of the prison but with the question of after-care.

Even more thought was being given by the government to the organisation and activities of the voluntary societies attached to prisons. The introduction of hard labour in 1776 and the system of payment by earning marks had applied only to men serving short sentences in local prisons, and not to inmates of convict prisons. The associations therefore attempted to assist convicts and recidivists, and administered monies left in bequests and wills specifically for this purpose.

Various modifications of the Act of 1776 had been made, including the provision of free transport from the prison to the parish in which the prisoner had been born—which was, in theory at least, responsible for him out of the rates. Another amendment allowed the Justices to pay a discharged prisoner a further amount of money if he remained in employment for twelve months after discharge—enough incentive for many to be of good behaviour for that time at least. The Discharged Prisoners' Act of Sir Robert Peel, passed in 1824, provided that all prisoners should be given a small sum of money from public funds on discharge, either to return to their native parish or to travel to wherever they might find work.

It is from the date of Peel's Act that the multiplicity of societies devoted to aiding prisoners really begins, and each society had different ways of achieving its aims.

Thus at Birmingham the Discharged Prisoners Society not only found respectable lodgings for ex-prisoners but also canvassed employers who might be willing to provide work for them. Worcester had a similar association by 1840, and here not only did they try to find employment but actually paid the prisoner a small unemployment benefit until he was suited. Gloucester had its Refuge for Discharged Prisoners in 1856 which boarded them free for up to a month while they sought work, whilst Wakefield went one better and provided work in its own Industrial Home, where the ex-prisoner could also live.

London's societies included the London Reformatory, the Preventive & Reformatory Institute and the Metropolitan Industrial Reformatory, the last mainly for the benefit of London's first all-women prison at Brixton. Throughout the country over 100 voluntary aid societies were at work, and although in theory they had been supervised by a central committee since 1878, this body had no real power or organising ability.

As public funds were now involved, the government in 1895 set up the Gladstone Committee which later issued a preliminary report on the associations. Predictably it found an unsatisfactory situation and 'a great want of uniformity in the work of the Societies and their methods'. The Prison Commissioners were thereupon urged to do something about putting their house in order, and in 1896 appointed their own committee of enquiry, headed by the Rev G. P. Merrick, Chaplain of Holloway Prison.

Merrick confirmed most of the findings of the Gladstone Committee and recommended to the Prison Commissioners revised rules for the prisoners' aid societies which included the regular submission of balance-sheets. He also urged that members of these societies should be allowed to visit prisoners just before release in order to make arrangements for employment where possible and to contact their families.

Though Merrick's recommendations were mainly based on the work of the societies, the repercussions were much wider and resulted in a major examination of prison administration in the London area. It was found that the capital's most modern prison, Wormwood Scrubs, was working under capacity. It also produced evidence of the difficulties being encountered by having special blocks set aside for women in the prisons of Brixton (by then a mixed remand prison), Pentonville and Wandsworth.

The Report of the Prison Commissioners for 1900 dealt with this problem. It suggested that women should no longer go to these prisons, but that Holloway's male population should be transferred to Wormwood Scrubs, and that Holloway should become 'women only' to streamline the administration. The Home Office agreed, and in February 1902 the prison entered upon its new role.

4
WOMEN ONLY

The decision to make Holloway a prison only for women was part of an administrative streamlining which affected many aspects of prison life and work. Of paramount importance was the establishment of a single code of prison rules which applied equally to 'local' and convict prisons, yet which could be altered, as the need arose, by the Secretary of State.

One change which affected Holloway was the right of short-term prisoners to remission of part of their sentence for good behaviour, a privilege until then allowed only to convicts awaiting penal servitude.

At the same time, in view of its all-female status, Holloway began to receive a very much more varied intake of prisoner than hitherto and developed into the multi-category prison which it has remained ever since.

The year 1902 also marked the Coronation of Edward VII and the end of the Boer War. Nearer home, in the new catchment area that Holloway now had more local changes were coming about. In 1900 London's underground railway system had been electrified and the Central London Line opened. Though horses were still the main source of energy for haulage motor-buses were beginning to appear, and it was not long before the new electric trams began to bump and sway along the Camden Road past the prison gates on their way to the Nag's Head and Holloway Road. Some conveniences which we customarily associate with the twentieth century had their roots firmly planted in the nineteenth. By the time Holloway became an all-female prison, for example, it had been possible to speak to Paris by telephone for over a decade. Other conveniences of the time are, unfortunately, no longer with us—such as no less than twelve postal deliveries daily in central London and up to half-a-dozen in the suburbs.

The majority of Holloway's inmates from 1902 knew little of these manifestations of gracious living. These women were largely the products of the East End sweat-shops, forced to petty thieving to support their children, the prostitutes who infested the dark alleys of Whitechapel and Houndsditch, the baby-farmers (such as the notorious Mrs Dyer of Reading) whose infant charges unaccountably died once they had been insured. And, of course, the drunks, the brothel-keepers and the vagrants who figure so largely in the statistics of the times. Two-thirds of Holloway's inmates in the first decade of the century were serving sentences for prostitution or drunkenness, and the rate of recidivism was appallingly high. An analysis of prisoners in Holloway, quoted by Sir Evelyn Ruggles-Brise, indicates that 75 per cent of the women admitted during 1910 had previously served prison sentences, and that during a period of three years 1,628 women incurred a total of 30,986 convictions for drunkenness. A selected group of 25 women first convicted for drunkenness in 1913 had, by the end of 1915, amassed a total of 353 convictions.

With both drunkenness and prostitution it was virtually impossible that a prison sentence should have any remedial effect. Yet in Holloway's first few years as a female penitentiary the number of individual women being sentenced fell, while the number of times the same women returned to prison increased. Ruggles-Brise comments on the difficulties of rehabilitation of women who have 'fallen from their high estate of probity and virtue', but the truth of the matter was that, at the time, such women had not very far to fall. Brought up in an atmosphere of abject poverty, theft and petty crime, 'probity and virtue' were qualities of which they could mostly know little enough. To earn a living on the streets was easy enough—to secure forgetfulness and oblivion in drink with the money earned was even easier. The most important part of any rehabilitation process, as anyone working amongst such women was by now becoming aware, is the willingness of the person concerned to alter her way of life. The prostitute in particular is not likely to be convinced that she is a 'fallen woman', and bitterly resents the implication of immorality. She feels she is supplying a social need and getting paid for it, and no moralising from the sex that ensures the continuance of her trade will make her change her mind.

It was for this reason that efforts to rehabilitate such women were considered likely to be more fruitful if conducted by women, rather than by prison chaplains or well-meaning male social workers. In 1901 the Lady Visitors' Association was founded, under the presidency of Adeline, Duchess of Bedford, and was described as 'a body of earnest and devoted ladies with experience of rescue-work and a keen sympathy with even the most degraded of their sex'. Working in close co-operation with the Visiting Committees and the Prison Commissioners, they organised systematic and regular visits to all prisoners in Holloway from the time of their admission to their discharge.

For the inmates of Holloway it was a welcome relief from the grinding monotony of their existence, for sixteen of the twenty-four hours of each day were spent in their cells. Meals were eaten there and most work done there, and the visit of anyone, effectual or ineffectual, was something to which every inmate looked forward. Chaplains were instructed to encourage prisoners to accept visits from the ladies of the Visitors' Association, and few needed the encouragement.

The introduction of the Borstal system in 1908, after some years of experimentation, also had its effect on Holloway. The Committee of 1894, which had suggested further enquiries into the administration of prisons and the treatment of prisoners, had said most emphatically that 'The age when the majority of habitual criminals are made lies between the ages of 16 and 21.' This was no new discovery, though it was the first time it had been so forcibly expressed in an official government publication. As early as 1815 a colony at Stretton, in Warwickshire, had been founded by people worried about the effect of a prison sentence on a young man or boy of under twenty years of age. They had ingeniously invoked the use of an old statute by which young persons could be hired out for agricultural work, and persuaded the justices to let them have the care of young offenders and to try and make them honest and useful citizens whilst at the same time doing productive work on the land. How successful the system was is difficult to gauge, for it was adopted nowhere else, and interest in the reform of juveniles remained an unpopular topic for discussion in Parliament for many years. However, when Sir Evelyn Ruggles-Brise took over from du Cane in the last years of the century he made it clear from the outset that one of his prime considerations in the overhaul of the prison system was to be the treatment of the juvenile offender.

It so happened that at the village of Borstal, near the convict prison at Chatham, was an annexe to the prison that was only part-used. The idea was not to take young first offenders or petty criminals, but young hooligans, perhaps with several previous convictions, and to attempt to stop them from embarking on lives of crime beyond the point of no return.

This, it was hoped, would be achieved with what Ruggles-Brise called the 'individualisation' of the prisoner, mentally, morally and physically. Selected staff would treat each delinquent as an individual, something which he had probably

63

never experienced before, and to enlist the aid of physical drill, gymnastics and instruction of various kinds.

That the scheme finally gained acceptance is due to the tenacity and faith of Ruggles-Brise who, in the early years before 1908, received no official support for his ideas and worked in the dark with very few to assist him. It soon became apparent that the kind of transformation hoped for could not be encompassed within six or even twelve months, and Ruggles-Brise believed that in most cases it would take three years' Borstal training, with periodic release, before any good would come of it. Inevitably, girls and women between sixteen and twenty-one came into the category that would be suitable for Borstal training, and from 1908 such girls were sent to Aylesbury Prison, which thus became the first female Borstal Institution. Should they fail to benefit from the training, and get into further trouble whilst on parole, they were brought back to Holloway Prison in the care of what came to be known as the 'Borstal Recall Section'. Aylesbury has long since ceased to house any Borstal girls, and the Borstal Recall Section of Holloway has now been transferred to Bullwood Hall since 1972.

While Holloway was taking part in such experiments and concerning itself with the future of young female offenders as well as with its more numerous complement of drunks and prostitutes, its work was proceeding comparatively unpublicised. It was a very different type of offender that suddenly shot Holloway into the headlines in 1906 and kept it there more or less continuously until the outbreak of war in 1914.

In 1903 the redoubtable Emmeline Pankhurst established, in Manchester, an organisation called the Women's Social & Political Union. Its main objective was to win women the right to vote, but the way it went about achieving this objective was to create more division of opinion, more disruption in the nation's affairs and more bitterness of feeling than had been experienced since Parnell and the Irish Question over a decade earlier.

The association created by Mrs Pankhurst had not been the first by any means to voice the question of female suffrage. Ever since the Reform Bill of 1832 there had been occasional and half-hearted attempts to rouse public opinion on the issue. As the century wore on the constant raising of the subject and the formation of female suffrage societies here and there gradually began to impinge on the public consciousness. In 1851 Sheffield had formed its Association for Female Franchise, and during the next decade several such societies were formed up and down the country. They were supported not only by women but also by a minority of influential and thinking men, such as Gladstone, Disraeli, Mill, Labouchère, John Bright and the Christian Socialist Tom Hughes, to be joined by many others in due course. Queen Victoria herself, however, opposed the movement with a violence and tenacity surprising in one who, in the early days of her marriage, had kept her husband so firmly in his place, and who later was to attempt to stop her son, the Prince of Wales, from accepting any responsibility in affairs of state. Lady Amberley, who read a paper on female suffrage at the Mechanics Institute in Stroud, was castigated by the Queen later:

> The Queen is most anxious to enlist everyone who can speak or write or join in checking this mad, wicked folly of 'Woman's Rights' with all its attendant horrors, on which her poor feeble sex is bent, forgetting every sense of womanly feeling and propriety. Lady Amberley ought to get a *good whipping*.

It was not only the vote that was exercising the minds of a large number of women during those years. Florence Nightingale, in the Crimea, had demonstrated what a forthright and determined woman could do despite fierce male opposition, and later Elizabeth Garrett and Sophia Jex-Blake were to pioneer the entry of women into the medical profession.

The formation of the WSPU by Mrs Pankhurst marked the transition from peaceful methods of persuasion to more militant action. Until 1903 women workers for the cause had been termed suffragists. After 1903, when things began to develop on a scale no government could ignore, they were called suffragettes—a name said to have been coined by *The Daily Mail*.

The first suffragettes to suffer imprisonment were Christabel Pankhurst and a young factory-worker, Annie Kenney, who on 13 October 1905 disrupted a meeting at the Free Trade Hall, Manchester, addressed by Sir Edward Grey on behalf of the Liberal Party (soon to come to power), by the constant reiteration of the question 'Will the Liberal Government give women the vote?'

Charged with technical assault and obstruction Christabel was fined ten shillings or seven days' imprisonment, Annie five shillings or three days. They both refused to pay the fine and were duly consigned to Strangeways Gaol, Manchester, thus beginning the pattern of 'imprisonment rather than fine' that was to characterise the future activities of the suffragette movement for the next decade.

The following year, 1906, as a result of the great Liberal victory, the spearhead of the suffragette movement was transferred to London. Its main target was the Liberal leader, Herbert Asquith, and in June 1906 a party of women mainly from the East End of London and led by Theresa Billington and Annie Kenney demonstrated outside the Asquith residence in Cavendish Square. Refusing to leave, and after sundry scuffles with the police, Theresa, Annie and several of their followers were arrested and charged the following day at Marylebone Police Court. The cases were heard by the stipendiary magistrate, Paul Taylor, who sentenced Theresa and Annie to a fine of £10 each or two months' imprisonment, the other women to six weeks or an equivalent fine. All refused to pay and all departed to Holloway Prison, the first of a long line of suffra-

66

gettes to enter the grim portals. Paul Taylor is credited with having made the optimistic comment 'This must come to an end. I will bring it to an end.' Little did he know that it was merely the beginning.

The journey to Holloway in the Black Maria, each woman sitting in a tiny closed cubicle with no view outside, the vehicle stopping from time to time to collect drunks and prostitutes from other courts, is vividly described by Sylvia Pankhurst in her absorbing account, *The Suffragette Movement* (1931). Once at the prison the dreary process of dehumanisation began, for the women were placed in the Second Division, which meant virtually no privileges and the wearing of prison clothes decorated with broad arrows.

Early in 1907 the Liberal government was seriously embarrassed by another clash between the police and suffragettes when a body of ladies led by the elderly and aristocratic Mrs Despard, marching in procession to the House of Commons, was suddenly confronted by a posse of mounted police. Neither would give way, and the police rode into the column in an attempt to disperse it, thereby injuring several women and in the scuffle that followed arresting Mrs Despard. The women regrouped time and time again, the whole affair lasting two hours during which news of the battle spread like wildfire throughout London. Mrs Despard was charged and sent to Holloway, as were several members of a similar rally held a few weeks later, though in this clash the police were not mounted.

A sign that the government was beginning to understand the situation better was seen when these prisoners were all sentenced to the First Division. But the numbers were increasing, and on one day alone at this time Holloway received into its capacious maw no less than seventy-five suffragettes. Also sentenced were a sprinkling of men who had attempted to protect the women from the action of the police.

During the two years between 1908 and 1910, the activities of the suffragettes were more spectacular than dangerous. They included episodes such as the dropping of thousands of leaflets on London by Miss Matters, a noted balloonist, an attempt to hand King Edward VII a petition during the State Opening of Parliament, and the first instance of a suffragette chaining herself to the railings of No 10 Downing Street in 1909. (W. S. Gilbert, of Gilbert & Sullivan fame, remarked when he heard of this that he intended to chain himself to the railings of Queen Charlotte's Maternity Hospital and shout 'Babes for men!')

But though the suffragettes were still being viewed in many quarters with amused tolerance, the sentences imposed on them were gradually becoming longer. Contingent after contingent served terms in Holloway of six or eight weeks, giving interviews to the press on release about the abominable conditions prevailing within. It became obvious that Holloway was lagging far behind comparable prisons in other countries, and a curious byproduct of the suffragette movement was that the revelations made by these articulate, unafraid women gradually resulted in an improvement in conditions in Holloway and in the treatment of women prisoners generally.

It was during that same year of 1909 that a comparatively new recruit to the cause succeeded in precipitating in Holloway what became one of the prison's most unpleasant and degrading episodes—the use of forcible feeding.

She was Marion Wallace-Dunlop, a Scottish authoress and painter, who in June 1909 had been sentenced to a month in Holloway for painting suffragette slogans on the walls of the House of Commons at night. She was sentenced to the Second Division, but warned the governor that she would go on hunger-strike unless re-allocated to the First Division as a political prisoner. The governor, of course, had no power to interfere with the sentence of the court, and on 5 July Marion began her hunger-strike.

The idea was evidently her own, and had not been discussed with other suffragettes, but it was undoubtedly effective, a ploy that was to embarrass both the government and the prison staff for some time to come. On this first occasion, however, after Miss Wallace-Dunlop had starved for four days and refused to eat the most tempting fare ever supplied to a prisoner in any category in Holloway, she was released—fainting and in a state of near-collapse but triumphant. It was not a triumph the government relished. After several other suffragettes had adopted the same tactics and gained their release the Home Secretary took action. Instructions went to the governors of all prisons that they must resort to the forcible feeding of prisoners on hunger-strike.

The first victim was Mrs Mary Leigh, well known to the police as the first suffragette to damage property (other than the breaking of windows), for she had climbed on to a building in Liverpool and hurled slates on to the roof of an adjoining hall where a political meeting was being held. She was in many ways a tough character, strong and courageous, and even after four days of fasting, and with her hands handcuffed behind her for thirty hours, it took the combined efforts of three wardresses and the prison doctor to force food down her. This was accomplished by administering 'nourishing food' in liquid form down the throat or via the nostrils by rubber tubes with the use of a stomach-pump in reverse. The degrading procedure had, until then, been used only in mental hospitals and only in extreme cases.

Once the news of this treatment leaked out, there was an immediate uproar throughout the country. Evidence was obtained from the medical press of such treatment resulting in serious damage to the oesophagus and intestines, and to the real possibility of death itself by this means. A petition of over 100 eminent physicians and surgeons urged the Home Secretary to stop the practice immediately, but Herbert Gladstone took refuge behind the Prison Commissioners and the famous 'Standing Orders', conduct which the *British Medical Journal* described as 'contemptible'.

By 1910 a change of government was obviously on the way

and this, together with the death of King Edward, resulted in a quietening of active militancy for a period. Trouble broke out again in 1912, on Mrs Pankhurst's return from America, when at four o'clock on a Friday afternoon in March suffragettes, acting as one, succeeded in breaking virtually every plate-glass window in Piccadilly, up Regent Street and along the greater part of Oxford Street, with hammers hidden in their muffs. The public were indignant, and clamoured for reprisals. Once again the Black Marias unloaded their cargoes of suffragettes at the reception area of Holloway, over 200 in all, and warrants were issued for the arrest of Mrs Pankhurst and her committee on charges of conspiracy. One of those who went to Holloway was the famous composer Dame Ethel Smyth, who had written a song for the suffragette movement. On one occasion, during exercise at Holloway, the entire contingent of suffragettes broke into song, Dame Ethel being observed at the window of her cell conducting the singing with a tooth-brush.

Mrs Pankhurst and her associates, after trial at the Old Bailey, were sentenced to nine months' imprisonment despite the jury's recommendation for leniency 'on account of the undoubtedly pure motives behind the agitation'. And the stores concerned later sued the participants for damage to their windows!

The problem of what to do with suffragettes in Holloway who went on hunger-strike was intended to be resolved by the introduction in 1913 of the Prisoners (Temporary Discharge) Act—the famous 'Cat & Mouse' Act. It laid down that any prisoner showing signs of ill-health through malnutrition could be released, but should be re-arrested if she did not comply with certain regulations. Later that year one of the leading suffragettes, Miss Emily Davison, threw herself under a horse during the Derby of 4 June and was killed. The affair caused a sensation, heightened by the fact that it was the King's horse that was involved, though this was pure chance. Emily

Davison herself, though a staunch and loyal worker in the background of the movement, was by no means a highly militant suffragette and her action seemed completely out of character to those who knew her. Crowds lined the streets to watch the funeral procession. Mrs Pankhurst, recently released from Holloway under the 'Cat & Mouse' Act, was about to step into her carriage and join the procession when she was re-arrested and returned to prison for taking part in this 'demonstration'. Her empty carriage, with drawn blinds, followed the coffin.

This pernicious Act did little to stem the activities of the most militant suffragettes. Nor did it stop the practice of forcible feeding, though it was invoked when resistance to such feeding began to affect the health of the prisoner. One young woman in Holloway, Mary Richardson, when asked by the prison doctor if she would refrain from militancy on release, replied that she would continue her activities and risk force-feeding as long as she could stand and see. 'They cannot do more than kill me,' she added. The official attitude to this matter is demonstrated in the doctor's answer: 'Unfortunately, it is not a question of killing you. You will be kept here until you are a skeleton and a nervous and mental wreck, and then you will be sent to an institution where they look after mental wrecks.'

This same Mary Richardson was the leader of the senseless attack on the nation's art treasures during 1913 and the early weeks of 1914, which did much harm and included damage to the Rokeby Venus in the National Gallery. This outbreak was the culmination of the worst period of militancy which had begun in 1912 and had resulted in Holloway being reduced to near-chaos. The prison was overflowing with suffragette prisoners who had dropped flaming rags into letterboxes, planted bombs in strategic places all over London including St Paul's and attacked politicians physically and viciously. Lloyd George, a prime target of the suffragette's venom, had a steel spike thrown through the window of his car which just missed his eye and entered his cheek. One of the glasshouses at Kew was destroyed and many empty properties were set on fire. Two suburban railway stations were practically destroyed. Though Mrs Pankhurst was by then spending the major part of her time in Holloway, the campaign continued to be organised by Christabel, who had fled to Paris. Sylvia, another daughter, went into hiding in the East End of London and transmuted her sister's orders into actions.

As 1914 advanced it became obvious that international affairs were becoming far more important than female franchise. The activities of the suffragettes declined, though some continued the campaign right up to the outbreak of war in August of that year. Towards the end of the war the Electoral Reform Bill of 1917 had taken the first step towards women's franchise by giving the vote to women over 30 years of age. The Sex Disqualification Act of 1919 allowed women to fill positions that had been impossible before, including becoming magistrates in the local courts. Those terrible weeks in Holloway had been worth-while after all, though many people were of the opinion that it was the work women had done during wartime that finally persuaded the government to give them the vote, rather than the peacetime sabotage and violence of Emily Pankhurst and her friends. Certainly the Pankhurst family were not united by their success, and their later history is a tragic one of accusations and recriminations which divided mother from daughter and sister from sister in a manner far removed from the single-mindedness of their suffragette days.

5

FAMOUS NAMES—AND
RECIDIVISTS

The activities of the suffragettes and their treatment in Holloway created several problems which were to have a significant
effect on prison administration as a whole in later years. From
1906, with suffragettes constantly in and out of prison, com-
parison became inevitable with the very different type of
regular female offender—the drunks, the prostitutes, the
thieves and brothel-keepers—whose failure to benefit from
frequent incarceration in Holloway was as great as that of the
suffragettes, but for other and less laudable reasons.

In 1908 an attempt to deal with these 'habitual offenders'
(as defined by the Prevention of Crime Act) was made by
allowing the courts to impose a sentence of 'preventive detention', which was to begin immediately *after* the normal period
of imprisonment was ended. A distinction was drawn between
the habitual offender who was merely a nuisance, and women
whose wrongdoings constituted a danger to society and the
state.

In 1912 part of Aylesbury Prison, in Buckinghamshire,
already in use as a female convict prison, was set aside for this
purpose. Few magistrates, however, seemed inclined to impose
a further and consecutive prison sentence on a woman who had

just completed her term, and in the following sixteen years only eleven such women were sent to Aylesbury. The magistrates felt, no doubt, that most women recidivists had only 'nuisance value' and were therefore not eligible for this treatment, and that those who constantly transgressed in matters serious enough to be classified as endangering society needed medical treatment rather than a further term of preventive detention.

Another scheme, running side-by-side with this one, had been in operation since 1905 and was rather more successful. This was the establishment of a Long Service Division by which women who had completed $7\frac{1}{2}$ years of a prison sentence were allowed certain privileges, including increased earnings in prison, the right to take meals 'in association' with other prisoners and permission to talk together at certain times. This may not have done much to help in the rehabilitation of the prisoner once she was released, but it certainly made her life in prison easier and gave her the opportunity of putting a little money away against the day of her release.

Of the 'nuisance' prisoners who formed the bulk of Holloway's population, by far the greatest number were the alcoholics. Aylesbury had become a female convict prison in 1896 and from 1902 had worked in very close co-operation with Holloway. A special block, known as the Female Inebriate Reformatory, had been built at Aylesbury, separated by a wall from the rest of the prison, and it regularly took the incorrigible alcoholics from Holloway. Unfortunately they were given no treatment and no employment, and any hope of treating alcoholism by such negative means was doomed to failure. Once again the magistrates of the country saw less and less point in sending these unfortunate women to Aylesbury, and by 1917 the Reformatory had only two 'inebriates' left in it. The space left free was used for the more practical purpose of housing women enemy aliens.

Other women who began merely as a nuisance but who later became important enough to endanger the security of the state were the unrepentant prostitutes. During peacetime, prostitutes had been looked upon mainly as a social menace and risk to health. But in wartime it was a very different matter, and from the outbreak of war in 1914 the authorities became very conscious of the fact that soldiers coming home on leave and consorting with prostitutes could well acquire venereal disease and so become unfit for combat.

Under the many provisions of the Defence of the Realm Act (the famous DORA beloved of the cartoonists of the Great War and after), any woman suspected of seeking the company of members of the Armed Forces could be taken into custody by the police and subjected to a medical examination. If VD were found, there was a maximum prison sentence of six months or a fine of £100. The over-enthusiastic manner in which certain members of the constabulary carried out their duties, often arresting perfectly respectable women and forcing them to submit to the indignity of tests, caused a national scandal, and the scheme did not last long. An even less practical idea was that women suspected of spreading VD should be restrained from 'frequenting or residing in military areas'.

One of the most bitter opponents of these parts of the Act was Dr Mary Gordon, appointed first Inspector of Women's Prisons in 1907. She realised the difficulties presented and the unfairness to women, quite apart from the ineffectiveness of the Act in stopping the spreading of disease by contact: in most cases the fines imposed were immediately paid by the 'ponce' and the girls went off to work again.

Dr Gordon brought a much-needed feminine view to the matter of women in prison. A year before she was appointed, Holloway had been enlarged by the addition of a further wing to accommodate 100 'Star' offenders. Dr Gordon inaugurated several ideas to make prison life more tolerable, including the provision of Swedish drill for all inmates, a form of exercise becoming very popular at the time, and creating a greater variety of work. She gave the menial tasks, such as scrubbing and cleaning, to the short-term inmates, reserving the more productive and interesting work for the long-term prisoners; in certain cases this consisted of training for some kind of work after release. It was under Mary Gordon's regime, and after revelations of conditions in Holloway made by the suffragettes, that lighting and ventilation in the cells was improved, with clear glass substituted for the opaque variety in the windows.

Though living conditions in Holloway were improved, the treatment of offenders, as laid down by the Home Office, came under severe criticism immediately after the war, largely as a result of the treatment of conscientious objectors. Dr Gordon associated herself with these criticisms, and the more enquiring attitude of the general public created a climate in which her demands for improvements were sympathetically heard. There were many who now accused Ruggles-Brise of being as outdated and inflexible as his predecessor, du Cane. Dr Gordon herself, after her retirement, was particularly outspoken, and compared British prisons unfavourably with those found in Europe, notably in France. Only in Britain, she maintained, 'were the criminal, feeble-minded, drunken, the early dement, the paranoic and the senile, the crippled and the young offender, all gathered together under the one prison system'.

This was, perhaps, unfair to Ruggles-Brise, who to give him his due had worked hard and with little official support to establish the Borstal system with which his name will always be associated. Nevertheless, Dr Gordon and many others felt that he should have done more to improve conditions in the existing penitentiaries, whilst by no means belittling what were the first real attempts made to rehabilitate young offenders before they started on the downward slope to adult criminality.

However, the public were now very much aware of what being in prison was like. They disliked the insinuation that anything French, even a prison, could possibly be better-run than the equivalent at home, and demanded to know why. In 1919 the government Research Department bowed to public opinion and set-up a Prison Enquiry Committee. Their report was not encouraging and, amongst other strictures, accused the Prison Commissioners of being 'as autocratic and irresponsible' as they had been in du Cane's day.

Yet, in addition to his Borstal work, Ruggles-Brise had been campaigning for many years for a more enlightened treatment of female short-term prisoners and had constantly pointed-out the inhumanity of treating men and women in prison in exactly the same way (with the exception of hard labour for women). He had stressed the physiological and emotional differences between men and women in their reaction to prison life, and how much more women suffered mentally than men. Although Mary Gordon had criticised his regime, both she and Ruggles-Brise had been fighting for the same cause through successive governments whose wish to improve prison conditions before the Great War was influenced by the possible loss of votes from those of the electorate who clung to the 'hang 'em-and-flog 'em' mentality. In 1921 Ruggles-Brise retired and later that year published his book *The English Prison System* (printed at HM Prison, Maidstone), in which he described the state of the prison system as he found it in 1892 and the situation when he left it nearly thirty years later.

The new Prison Commissioner was Sir Maurice Waller, and once again another new broom had some sweeping to do. In 1922 clothing for women prisoners was improved, the convict-crop for men done away with, and for both men and women prisoners the notorious broad-arrow on clothes and property was finally abolished.

During the first twenty years of its existence as a women-only prison, Holloway gained that reputation for drama within its walls which made it world-famous and which has never really left it. In 1910, as the suffragette movement was already beginning to make the name of the prison known, Holloway received a prisoner who was destined to achieve a permanent place in the annals of crime from her association with one of the most famous murderers of all time—Hawley Harvey Crippen. Her name was Ethel le Neve, and she was the friend of the little American doctor who murdered his domineering wife, Belle Elmore, at his house in Hilldrop Crescent just round the corner from Holloway Prison.

Six weeks after Mrs Crippen's disappearance Ethel le Neve came to live with the doctor in Hilldrop Crescent and, during that period, must have often wondered just what sort of women were locked up behind the castellated walls of the great fortress which she could see so plainly from the house. She was not to be left in doubt for long. Soon after, disguised as a boy, she was crossing the Atlantic with her lover, only to be arrested off the coast of Newfoundland by a Scotland Yard detective—the first case of a murderer being arrested by means of the new radio-telegraph. Brought back to this country, Ethel herself became an inmate of Holloway during the period of Crippen's trial at the Old Bailey which resulted in his conviction and subsequent execution at Pentonville in November 1910.

At her own trial Ethel le Neve was acquitted of complicity and released. Early in 1911 she emigrated to Canada where she lived under an assumed name for more than fifty years. As an old lady she returned to England in 1962 and died in Croydon in 1965, where she was living with relatives. According to reports, from the day of her release from Holloway in 1910 until the day she died, she never once mentioned Crippen or anything to do with the affair.

In 1912, two years after the Crippen case, the wife of another murderer was also held in Holloway during her husband's trial. This was Mrs Seddon, who, with her husband Frederick, was charged with the murder by arsenic of their lodger, Miss Eliza Barrow, at their home in Kentish Town. Seddon himself was sentenced to death and executed at Pentonville but Mrs Seddon was acquitted at her own trial a month later.

In both these cases the man was hanged, the woman playing only a minor part in the affair. But in 1923 Holloway had a prisoner whose trial, conviction and subsequent execution for the murder of her husband in collaboration with her lover was a *cause célèbre* throughout the civilised world. This was Edith Thompson, an imaginative and flirtatious young woman of 28, who in October 1922 was walking with her husband in a dark road in Ilford, Essex, when a figure came from the shadows and stabbed him to death. The assailant was later proved to be Frederick Bywaters, a ship's purser and Edith's lover, who had once been a lodger at the house.

From the moment of her arrest Edith Thompson denied all complicity in the matter, and insisted that she had no idea that Bywaters was anywhere in the vicinity or had any intention of harming her husband, a contention that was also confirmed by Bywaters himself. Nevertheless, damaging correspondence was produced at the trial at the Old Bailey which appeared to indicate that Edith had been studying the action of poisons whilst her lover was at sea, and was constantly asking him to 'send something' to her which would make her free of her husband. There was equally strong evidence that Edith Thompson lived in a world of fiction and make-believe, and even her comment in one letter to Bywaters that she had actually fed broken glass to her husband was proved later to be a pure fabrication when the post-mortem on Thompson was carried out by Sir Bernard Spilsbury.

Despite this, after the five-day trial that followed, she was convicted of complicity in the murder by stabbing of her husband, and she and Bywaters were sentenced to death. Bywaters remained comparatively unmoved at his own fate, but the shock to Edith was more than she could bear. She was returned to the hospital wing of Holloway in a state of collapse while arrangements were made for an appeal to be lodged against sentence. On 21 December 1922 the appeal was heard by Lord Hewart, Lord Chief Justice of England, sitting with

Mr Justice Salter and Mr Justice Darling. None could find any reason for allowing the appeal and the findings of the court were confirmed.

The case had aroused world-wide controversy and there had been a good deal of criticism of the summing-up of Mr Justice Shearman which was said to have been biased against Edith Thompson more on moral than on criminal grounds. There were many in the country who were shocked and horrified that her appeal had not been allowed. The Home Secretary was inundated with petitions in respect of both the accused— Bywaters by virtue of his youth and his sudden and allegedly unpremeditated action in stabbing Thompson when he confronted him on that tragic evening—and Edith, on the grounds that she took no part in the murder, or in the planning of it. The Home Secretary refused to alter the course of justice. On a raw January morning in 1923 Edith Thompson and Frederick Bywaters were hanged at the identical moment—he at Pentonville and she at Holloway.

The emotional atmosphere engendered by the case had reached fever heat, heightened by the drama of the appeal and the petition and the knowledge that it was fifteen years since a woman had been hanged in Britain. Immediately after the execution sensational and bizarre stories began to circulate concerning Edith Thompson's last minutes before her execution. *The Daily Express* reported how she had 'disintegrated as a human creature before she reached the scaffold. Other reports stated that she had fought and screamed every inch of the way to the gallows, requiring the combined strength of five warders to get her to the execution shed. There was the odd statement made by the wife of Ellis, the official hangman who had despatched Edith and 200 others besides in a long career and who committed suicide eight years later. Mrs Ellis said that hanging Edith Thompson had affected his mind and resulted in his final derangement. The Home Office, whilst denying that anything untoward had taken place, refused to comment on the matter, and for over thirty years the gruesome rumours continued. It was not until 1956, during a debate in the House of Commons on the death penalty, that an official announcement was made by the Home Secretary, Mr Gwilym Lloyd George, on the circumstances surrounding the hanging of Edith Thompson.

> Before the execution the governor of Holloway Prison who was also the Medical Officer (Dr. John H. Morton, who died in 1935), in accordance with the discretion vested in him, gave Mrs. Thompson sedatives.
> At the time of the execution the governor considered that it would be more humane to spare her the necessity of walking the few yards to the execution chamber, and although he thought that she could have walked without assistance he had her carried and she was supported on the scaffold.
> Apart from this nothing unusual occurred. Having examined all the information available I am satisfied that there is no truth in the allegation that Mrs. Thompson 'disintegrated as a human creature' or that she 'fought, kicked and screamed and protested her innocence to the last and that it required about five men to hold her down while being carried to the gallows and having the noose put over her', or in the story that her 'insides fell out'.
> No incident occurred during the execution of such a nature as to call for any change in the instructions to governors, and in fact no change was made in consequence of it.

After thirty-three years this assurance came a little late for many people, for during that period nine more women had been hanged in Britain, the last only a year before the pronouncement quoted above.

But women who murder, though guaranteed to command the greatest publicity, are comparatively rare, and most such women are first offenders. Far more important to the penologist is the recidivist, the habitual offender for whom prison has long since ceased to act as a deterrent—becoming, indeed, for some, a haven from a harsh and loveless world.

The Borstal system began as an experiment in the treatment of juvenile offenders who could be in danger of becoming habitual criminals, and seventy years later it is still operating in Britain. Curiously, it never received favour in America and no comparable method of dealing with juveniles has yet been established there.

The Borstal system, as a form of treatment and rehabilitation, is as applicable to girls as it is to boys. Several such institutions exist since Aylesbury became the first Borstal for women and girls, and a recent experiment is in operation at East Sutton Park near Maidstone, Kent, where an 'open' Borstal provides a compromise between security and loss of liberty. Holloway is not directly concerned with the Borstal system except that it has a Borstal 'recall' wing in the prison, where girls who have been in further trouble after release from Borstal are held, pending reallocation for further treatment.

However, a closer association with the system was established in 1973 when some twenty habitual offenders (all mature women) were sent from Holloway to the open Borstal at East Sutton Park to join the forty girls already there. At this stage it is difficult to say what success this regime is likely to have. While this kind of treatment for a young girl may be appropriate, it is possible that a woman who has already become institutionalised by successive sentences in prison may not respond, or may respond too well and be unwilling to leave and face the outside world again.

The regime at East Sutton Park is based more on rehabilitation therapy than on a custodial sentence, and the atmosphere is deliberately relaxed. Girls and women are encouraged to confide in the staff, none of whom are in uniform, and discuss their problems. For the prison officers concerned this poses certain problems, for while trying to obtain a girl's confidence there must be no suggestion of prying into her affairs. The staff are selected for tact and understanding, but their work is not made easier by the influx of students of sociology who from time to time arrive and appear to consider the place an experimental laboratory with the inmates as specimens. (When one sublimely tactless student, with no preliminaries, asked one of the inmates what she was 'in' for, the Borstal girl looked her coldly in the eye and replied 'For murdering a student of sociology'!)

Some girls do not adapt to the system of comparative freedom and seem frightened by it. For people like this, who cannot bring themselves to accept any responsibility and are insecure and disturbed, as for the older women who have seen too much of prison, the only solution is return to a closed Borstal or to Holloway.

Holloway, as can be seen, with its population of adult offenders, Borstal recalls, long-term and short-term inmates and habitual offenders, handles a very wide cross-section of all those women who find themselves in trouble. One of the categories, however, urgently requires a different form of treatment—the girl of between fourteen and seventeen years of age who is on remand while untried and unconvicted. Often these girls are taken into custody as a result of offences connected with drugs, with the added problem that frequently they have no fixed place of abode. The magistrates are then faced with the alternative of sending them to Holloway on remand—an unsatisfactory expedient under present conditions—or allowing them bail, giving the police and welfare officers the task of keeping track of them and ensuring their appearance in court later. The obvious solution is to send the girls to a hostel, but this is where the system breaks down. There are just not enough hostels. In a case at Clerkenwell Court in 1973 the stipendiary magistrate allowed bail to a teenage girl with the utmost reluctance, remarking that 'she would almost certainly wander off and get back on cocaine and heroin again'. She did. No suitable hostel

83

was able to accept the girl, and it was a straight choice between the risks inherent in bail or custody in Holloway.

Much of the trouble is caused by the provisions of the 1969 Children & Young Persons Act which abolished the distinction between approved schools, remand homes and homes for children under care, classifying all of them as 'community homes'. In addition it gave such establishments the power of refusing to take any child it thought unsuitable, though the responsibility for the welfare of the child rests fairly and squarely on the local authority in whose area the home is situated. Several cases have come to light where young children have had to be sent to prison because the community homes, on one pretext or another, refused to accommodate them.

One of the most disturbing cases was the girl of fourteen who spent almost the whole of 1973 in Holloway while a total of no less than thirty-seven community homes refused to accept her. During October and November 1973 a total of sixteen girls under the age of seventeen were in Holloway on remand. Although girls of this age are not in a cell, but accommodated in the hospital wing, the situation is disturbing. The effect that prison can have on a sophisticated adult is shattering enough, let alone on an impressionable teenager. And the prison hospital, where the girls are likely to be in the company of some of Holloway's less controlled inmates, can scarcely be described as 'a place of safety' within the meaning of the Act.

The alternative, since the 1969 Act came into force, is for the welfare or probation services to try and remedy the situation, allowing the girl to return to her own home even after conviction. This is self-defeating in many cases. The young offender, having been tried, found guilty and therefore expecting to have to undergo a form of training at a special centre, finds herself back home, in the same environment and probably attending the same school. This is because the welfare officers have nowhere suitable to send her. She can easily assume that authority is powerless and revert to her former activities, with

Page 85 (*above*) Edith Thompson, hanged at Holloway in January 1923; (*left*) the arrest of Mrs Christofi, hanged at Holloway in 1954 for the murder of her daughter-in-law

Page 86 (*above*) Holloway's famous 'centre' showing the radiating cell-blocks and galleries, 1947; (*below*) Sunday morning service in 1947

the added *cachet* of having an official police record. For many the progression from detention centre, through Borstal to prison, is a calculated ambition, and a means of climbing the anti-social ladder.

6

HOLLOWAY BETWEEN THE WARS

One of the provisions of the Defence of the Realm Act which had been imposed during the Great War had been the banning of the supply of intoxicating liquor after 10pm. While the Act itself lingered on, various amendments had been made affecting the licensing regulations, one of which was to allow the sale of alcohol until midnight as long as a meal was being consumed at the same time. This concession was later extended to 2am.

Despite the grim economic situation of post-war Britain, those with money took advantage of the swing away from wartime restrictions, and in London in particular the 1920s saw the development of the night-club racket. Licences for food and drink were granted to club owners whose business standards and morals were often questionable, and clubs proliferated alarmingly in the square mile of London's West End known as Soho.

These clubs, often in single rooms in Frith Street, Wardour Street, Charlotte Street and the area adjacent to Piccadilly and Shaftesbury Avenue, were mostly in dimly-lit and sleazy premises, with exorbitant prices charged for drinks and a plentiful supply of attractive girls (at least in the half-light) ready to persuade the customer to part with his money in the hope of 'entertainment' later.

Whilst most regulations were openly flouted, club proprietors made great use of the legal requirement that all persons supplied with drink should be paid-up members, and charged exorbitant sums for such 'membership' while conveniently ignoring the equally valid regulation that, even having paid a fee, the client did not legally become a member until forty-eight hours after acceptance.

Complaints from visitors became so numerous that the 'clip-joints' affair became a public scandal. The police, operating from Vine Street Police Station in the angle of Regent Street and Piccadilly, were virtually powerless, for no sooner was a club raided and struck-off than it changed its name and re-opened immediately, often in a different room in the same building. At one period there were estimated to be nearly 1,000 clubs in Soho, most of them operating illegally. In 1928 the police launched a campaign against them, using the newly-formed 'clubs branch' of the CID.

At that time the best-known personality in the world of London's night-clubs was Mrs Kate Meyrick, who had already clashed with the police three years earlier when she had persistently flouted the law in respect of the clubs she owned, and had served six months in Holloway as a result. On her release she had immediately opened other clubs, and by 1928 was recognised as the 'Night Club Queen' of London. Although instructed to clean-up the West End, the police were hampered by the fact that they had no power to enter a club without a warrant, and for this some proof of violation of the regulations was necessary. Both members of the CID and the uniformed branch in plain clothes were used to infiltrate clubs by becoming members, getting served with drinks illegally and so providing the evidence required.

The clubs owned by the charming Mrs Meyrick seemed singularly immune from attention. Though openly breaking almost every licensing regulation, Mrs Meyrick openly boasted that plain-clothes policemen visiting her clubs were always spotted, refused drinks and sent away with no evidence. Even when evidence was obtained and a raid arranged, everything was found to be in order and no drinks were visible after the permitted hours.

It became obvious that somebody with inside information was tipping her off regarding raids, and soon anonymous letters were being received at Scotland Yard implying that a Sergeant Goddard, a plain-clothes officer at Vine Street, was the go-between. Observation was kept on Goddard, and the accusations seemed justified when club after club due to be raided was warned in advance every time Goddard was involved in the arrangements. Finally a raid was organised on one of Mrs Meyrick's larger clubs, the fact being kept a closely guarded secret from Goddard. The police found the club in full operation long after the permitted hours, serving drinks to nearly 300 people, many well known in London society. Mrs Meyrick was arrested and eventually served another six months, leaving her clubs in the hands of her glamorous and well-connected daughters.

Goddard's private life was being investigated meanwhile, and it was soon found that he was living far beyond his means as a £6-a-week police sergeant, with a house worth £2,000 and a car valued at £400, all recently purchased for cash. Goddard explained these amounts away by saying he had been lucky at the races and had made a large profit from shares in the British Empire Exhibition at Wembley, but the police were not satisfied. Checks on his finances revealed that the sergeant had several safe-deposit boxes in his name and he was invited to reveal their contents. Goddard had no alternative, as the request came from the police Disciplinary Board, and sums of more than £12,000 were discovered. It did not take long to trace these notes back to Mrs Meyrick and various others, including the proprietors of two West End brothels.

Goddard, Mrs Meyrick and their associates were charged at the Old Bailey in January 1929 before Mr Justice Avory and found guilty by the jury after three hours' retirement. Goddard was dismissed the force, fined £2,000 and sentenced to eighteen months' imprisonment. Mrs Meyrick went through the entrance-gates of Holloway for the third time, on this occasion for a stay of eighteen months.

The post-war period also saw many changes in prison administration. Women prisoners were gradually removed from a number of provincial prisons, and by 1925 the main concentration was at Holloway and Manchester.

In 1927 Miss Mary Size was appointed the first woman deputy-governor of Holloway, under Dr John Hall Morton, an event of the greatest significance to the prison system as a whole.

Mary Size was a woman with long experience in the service. She had been in charge of the Borstal Institute at Aylesbury under its famous governor Dame Lillian Barker, and as the result of her achievements in this still largely experimental field had been appointed lady superintendent of Liverpool Prison in 1925.

Until Mary Size's Holloway appointment, the administration of the women's section of all prisons had been in the hands of male governors and assistants, though lady superintendents carried out their instructions. At Holloway Miss Size had a degree of responsibility and independence unknown before, an obviously desirable change in a prison with a population of nearly 600 women. Her position was made even stronger a few years later when Lilian Barker, her former colleague at Aylesbury, was appointed the first woman Prison Commissioner under its chairman, Sir Harold Scott.

At Holloway the staff of about 160 was divided into two sections, 'Discipline' and 'Nursing', with Miss Size responsible for the former. As a medical man, Dr Morton concerned himself mainly with health and hygiene in the prison and was the first governor to introduce nurses into the prison service.

Soon after Mary Size was appointed to Holloway came a curious incident which called for the combined resources of both the disciplinary and medical factions of the prison. This was the arrival of the notorious 'Colonel' Barker, a powerfully-built woman who for seven years had masqueraded as a man and who, at the time of her arrest, was employed as restaurant-manager of the Regent Palace Hotel. She had been arrested as the result of a warrant issued in connection with her non-appearance at bankruptcy proceedings and despite her protests was taken to Brixton Prison. The inevitable medical examination which followed soon revealed her true sex, and after an agitated governor of Brixton had telephoned Miss Size, the 'colonel' was hurriedly transferred to Holloway where she was received complete in male attire and in a state bordering on collapse. After great difficulty she was persuaded to change into prison clothing of a somewhat more feminine nature and remained on remand until her case came up. By the time she left prison a few days later the news of her escapades had reached a delighted public, and hundreds thronged the main gates of Holloway, together with press and photographers, awaiting this now nationally famous figure. Miss Size, in an attempt to avoid the publicity, guided the 'colonel' out through the back of the prison and over a fence into the adjacent Dalmeny Avenue. Unfortunately the press had found out about this plan and a battery of cameras faced the pair.

After the bankruptcy proceedings had been heard a great deal of evidence was produced about the 'colonel's' past life, including the interesting information that she had 'married' another woman some years before and thus laid herself open to a charge of making a false declaration to the registrar. Stories about the 'colonel' spread throughout Britain, the favourite joke of the time being that it was this episode that had started the custom of beginning business letters 'Dear Sir or Madam'!

Colonel Barker returned to Holloway to serve her sentence, but when released a few months later was able to leave the prison once again in male clothing, and with no one present to see her departure. Such is the shortness of public memory, and she was never heard of again.

With Lilian Barker to support her work, Mary Size began a gradual improvement in conditions at Holloway, long overdue. For the first time in penal history a woman in charge of women prisoners could discuss their problems with a woman commissioner and be free of male influence. There was much to be done.

The first impression made on a newcomer to Holloway varies considerably according to the conditions under which the visit is made. Most have described its appearance as 'grim' though some have thought it 'picturesque' and 'far from frightening'. In fact the newly-sentenced woman arriving in the prison van from court is hardly in a position to admire or deplore the more fanciful aspects of Bunning's architecture. She is more likely to be in a confused or even stunned state, her mind still filled with the shock of the sentence, worrying about the family she is leaving behind and with a blank and desolate future ahead of her of which she can know nothing. She is not, at that moment, aware of the organisations that can give her assistance in these problems. To quote Joan Henry's book *Who Lie in Gaol* (1952), 'Even to those who have been "inside" for ten years or more the first few hours of imprisonment are as indelibly printed on the mind as if they had happened only the day before.'

Small wonder that the Reception Area of Holloway, where the new arrival is registered, her belongings taken from her and listed, her clothing removed and exchanged for a voluminous white gown while awaiting her medical examination, is one of the most heartrending parts of the prison. Those in charge do the best they can within the limits of their work and exert a

93

sympathy and understanding that is a revelation to the on-
looker. It is not, after all, their fault if the new arrival must sit
waiting in a cubicle, frightened and alone, waiting for the doctor
to arrive. It is inevitable that it is here that the process of
complete depersonalisation begins—to many the most terrifying
aspect of prison life. It is here that the paradox first becomes
evident that the woman, though isolated from the outside world
and everything she knows, is never to be alone. Cubicles and
bathrooms are never locked and constantly supervised, and the
ever-present spy-hole in the cell door keeps her on view at any
time of day or night.

The 'centre' of the prison, that busy area from whence the
radiating arms of the cell-blocks lead away, is at first a confusing
jangle of sounds and sights as prisoners and staff pass to and
fro, clattering up and down the iron spiral stairways that lead
to the upper storeys. Latticed ironwork, smooth walls and an
impression of vast height surround the new arrival as she waits
to be conducted to her cell. That first night in prison is likely
to be the most miserable she will spend in her life.

But gradually the routine is assimilated. The early bell, the
making of her bed, the 'slopping-out' that has remained a
feature of the penal system for so long, slowly takes its place
with the routine of lining up for meals, the exercise in the yard
and the work that goes on daily. She even becomes acclimatised
to the constant jingling of keys, the slamming of heavy doors
and the never-ending echo that seems to accompany every
activity in Holloway. Gradually, perhaps, a crumb of comfort
is found in the realisation of how many other girls and women
are similarly placed. There will be more than a crumb of
comfort in the discovery that many prisoners seem cheerful and
relaxed and that the prison officers are human and certainly
not the ogres of popular imagination.

If Holloway is less depressing than is feared (and few prisons
are as grim inside as the public thinks) this is a legacy of the
work done by Mary Size and Lilian Barker in those early years

of the 1930s. One of the first actions of the two women was to inaugurate a complete scheme of redecoration, carried out by the prisoners themselves, substituting shades of cream and green for the drab orange and brown that had been the standard colour-scheme before. Walls were demolished here and there and larger rooms created, the heavy manual work being done by specially-selected male prisoners from Pentonville. The old condemned cell (which from the time of Edith Thompson's execution was said to be haunted) was demolished and the area cleared for a store. The chapel (until then used for all denominations) was completely renovated, and at a later stage an outbuilding was converted, under the personal guidance of Miss Size, to make a Roman Catholic church which was dedicated by Cardinal Hinsley.

In the cells (though even that word was disappearing from use) women could put up posters and pictures and have photographs of their children and families (though, unaccountably, not of animals). Outside the prison buildings the grounds were improved by the planting of flower-beds, though this was no easy task in the confined, wedge-shaped spaces between the radiating arms of the cell-blocks.

Young prisoners, in particular, benefitted from the action of these two enlightened women. Regular tuition was begun in home nursing, hygiene and the management of children, and outside lecturers were brought in to talk on current affairs and other topics. Handicraft classes were begun, the results of which were proudly displayed at the annual exhibition and, with the help of the Pentonville prisoners, a bowling-green was constructed for use by the older women.

Not that all this was accomplished without opposition, much of it from the older prison officers in the prison itself. Though Mary Size and Lilian Barker could give instructions as to what was to be done, this did not always ensure that it was carried out. Mysterious difficulties arose, often raised by the diehard core of officers opposed to what they considered the 'mollycoddling' of prisoners. Written orders unaccountably vanished in the maze of prison administrative red tape. To many of the older prison officers the concept of working *with* the prisoners was wholly alien. They had been trained in a system which involved the constant humiliation of the prisoner as a reminder of her sins, an attitude which survived far longer than the Commissioners realised and of which traces persist to this day.

But though the walls might be painted cream, though girls were taught to make soft toys and learn about the outside world, Holloway was still Holloway. The very architecture of the place was a constant reminder of the Victorian penitentiary and House of Correction, even if the original intention of making it 'a place of terror to evil-doers' no longer applied. And though every prisoner waited anxiously for her release, for many there was the constant and nagging fear of what was to happen once they gained their freedom.

In this connection the work of the voluntary visitors cannot be too highly stressed. They were constantly on duty in the prison, comforting and advising, and did much to make life more tolerable for those willing to accept their friendship. That they did so with such success, without earning the reputation of being bumbling do-gooders, is more remarkable when one finds the high number of titled ladies doing this work—ladies who must have had a very limited understanding of the sort of conditions the average prisoner lived in outside and of the circumstances that had resulted in imprisonment in Holloway. Lady Mary Carter, for example, a dedicated voluntary visitor for many years, has written what seems at times to be a rather starry-eyed account of life in Holloway, *A Living Soul in Holloway* (1938), with her talk of 'inviting menus' of golden sponge pudding and 'delicious ship's cocoa'! One tends to wonder just how much ship's cocoa Lady Mary had drunk in her time! (In fact it was so unpopular that it was *discontinued* soon after.) Her account is certainly at variance with the description of prison life by Joan Henry and most other ex-prisoners who have written about their experiences. Yet it was Lady Carter and two friends who, in 1922, formed what was to be one of the most important ancillary services to Holloway ever devised—the Holloway Discharged Prisoners' Aid Society. Whatever the value of the prison visits, it was without doubt the work done in the rehabilitation of prisoners that was the greatest achievement.

A hostel was opened near the prison, in Dalmeny Avenue, where discharged prisoners could live and be cared for while efforts were made to house them permanently and find them employment. They were clothed and fed, often given training in a trade and employment found for them. The Thirteen Counties Scheme (as it came to be called from the original catchment area of Holloway) received financial support from a variety of sources once its work became known. The City Livery Companies responded nobly, perpetuating the long connection of the City with their original House of Correction from 1852. The Salvation Army, the Church Army and religious bodies of almost every denomination accepted girls from the Holloway hostel into their own hostels, while other smaller and private organisations, such as the Queen Mary Needlework Guild, provided regular supplies of clothing or quietly settled outstanding bills incurred by families while the mother was in prison.

This real, solid help moved Dr William Temple, when Archbishop of Canterbury, to say: 'I do not think there is any work on which we can with greater confidence invoke the blessing of Almighty God. We are terribly apt to think that somehow or other prison work takes care of itself, and that we of the general public have no responsibilities in connection with it. This is not so, even within the prison walls, and very markedly indeed is it not so when prisoners are leaving prison and returning to civil life.'

One important innovation of the 1930s at Holloway was the introduction of an earnings scheme, first experimented with at

Wakefield Prison. Those eligible could earn from 10d a week rom their first eight weeks in prison, rising to a maximum of 4s. This money the prisoner could save, or spend in the new canteen or the 'shop' set up in a disused cell where goods from local shops were displayed, on a 'sale or return' basis.

The scheme was a huge success and played a considerable part in improving morale. Miss Size recalls how, soon after the system started, an excited prisoner informed her that this was the first time for years that she had handled money honestly obtained! It also allowed prisoners to buy cosmetics for the first time. Previously the idea of a woman in prison being allowed to use even the most elementary kind of make-up had been unthinkable. It took a woman to realise just what a psychological blow the banning of cosmetics was, something that no man would have understood. It also ended the traffic in smuggled cosmetics brought in by visitors and the ingenious attempts to improvise from materials at hand, such as the soaking of exercise-book covers to obtain rouge for lipsticks and the use of boot-polish as a substitute for mascara.

Further improvements in the wellbeing of prisoners came with the abolition of the old wooden planks used with mattresses and their replacement by conventional iron bedsteads with springs. Lights-out was put back to 10pm, allowing women to read or write in their cells after the day's work was done.

Under Dr Morton great attention had been paid to improving conditions in the hospital wing, and this continued after his sudden death in 1935. By now the hospital staff consisted almost entirely of State Registered nurses who were also certified midwives, and the standard of care provided was equal to anything obtainable in an outside hospital. Illness, on the whole, was comparatively rare in Holloway, for most inmates were leading a far more regular life than they had ever done before and were probably eating better. The mental ills that beset women in prison are a very different matter and will be discussed elsewhere.

An important part of the work done by the nursing staff was the care of babies born in Holloway. Here again, the infants probably got off to a better start than would have been possible under home conditions. Pre-natal care was given and, after confinement, training in infant care and hygiene. On discharge each mother with a baby born in Holloway was given a complete new outfit for the child.

But despite all these innovations the complete modernisation of Holloway was impossible as long as it continued to be housed in the vast Victorian building. By then both prison officers and staff had become infected with the enthusiasm engendered by Mary Size and Lilian Barker, but all were battling against insuperable odds. Lilian Barker began to campaign for the demolition of the building and the provision of a new women's prison near London where her progressive ideas could be used to full capacity. But the attitude of the Treasury was not helpful. As long as Holloway was functioning efficiently, any expenditure on a new prison could only be given very low priority in future budgets. It was, in fact, the very enthusiasm of Lilian Barker and the reforms and improvements that she and Mary Size had brought about in Holloway that militated against their arguments for a new prison. It was an ironical situation, despite the fact that the Treasury was well aware that only three new prisons had been built in Britain since Wormwood Scrubs in 1874. (These were: Bristol, 1883; Camp Hill, 1892 and Norwich, 1912.)

Not until 1937 did there seem to be any hope. In that year Sir Samuel Hoare became Home Secretary; as great-nephew of the reformer Elizabeth Fry, he had always taken a keen interest in prison administration, and was known to be sympathetic to Lilian Barker's pleas. The result of Hoare's appointment was that the Criminal Justice Bill of 1938 included provision for an extensive programme of prison rebuilding, with Holloway having top priority. Lilian Barker and her colleagues were delighted, and began to draw up plans based on her ideas

99

of a 'model' prison for women outside London. Her views can best be summarised in her remark that 'instead of parking women in prison I should like to imprison them in a park'—an attitude far in advance of those of many keen reformers of the day. In view of the undoubted success of her work at Aylesbury, where for the first time in years the great double-gates of the prison had been left permanently open and the girls encouraged to work in the fields, her opinions were valued. The Prison Commissioners went to work, and submitted plans acceptable to the Treasury and to the Home Office. A site was found near London at Heathrow (on ground which is now part of the runway of London Airport), with provision for a Borstal Institution adjoining.

But 1938 was not a good year for new planning projects. The Munich crisis showed how near to war Britain was, and what planning went forward was concerned more with defence than with penology. All schemes for a new prison were shelved and Holloway, in common with the rest of Britain, began to prepare for war.

When it finally came, on 3 September 1939, Holloway and its staff had already been training in civil defence, air raid precautions and the building of shelters. Plans were also ready for evacuation, and immediately war was declared the Home Secretary announced that all prisoners with three months or less of their sentence to run should be immediately discharged. This was accomplished at Holloway within forty-eight hours and involved the release of some 200 women and girls. The long-term prisoners, about seventy in number, together with staff, were evacuated to Aylesbury Prison, forty miles from London, from which most of the Borstal girls had been discharged under the same Order.

Conditions at Aylesbury were far from good, for there had been little time to arrange the transfer and much of the accommodation had been out of use for some years. But once again the indefatigable Mary Size went into action, and with working parties scrubbing, clearing and decorating, the few remaining Borstal girls were moved to what had been the former Inebriate Reformatory.

Scarcely had this been accomplished when the population of the prison began to be increased by the arrival of women detained under Regulation 18B which covered actions 'prejudicial to the conduct of the war' but had gathered into its net many whose actions were 'prejudicial' merely because they were of alien origin. Understandably some of these women were at first difficult to handle. As with the males detained under 18B on the Isle of Man, they were embittered by the action of the British government in interning people who had fled from Germany precisely to escape that fate at Nazi hands. Illusions regarding the freedom and tolerance to be found in Britain were shattered, the result being a sullen defiance of authority in prison and a refusal to co-operate.

Gradually, however, they found that it was to their benefit to take part in the normal prison activities, not from fear of reprisals but rather from fear of boredom, and something approximating to the routine that had been established at Holloway came into being under very different circumstances at Aylesbury. The work of the staff during this period was greatly eased by the assistance of many local people and the personal interest they showed in the work of the prison. This was something natural to those who lived in a country town, but was rare in a big city.

In 1942 it was decided to move all prisoners back to Holloway, a decision regretted by staff and prisoners alike, and the rural phase of the prison's history came to an end. The following year Miss Size retired from the prison service, her health having suffered from the strain of work, though she continued to serve with the Red Cross for the remainder of the war. In 1946 this remarkable woman emerged from retirement to become governor of the first open prison for women at Askham Grange, near York.

7
THE LAST YEARS

Although the outbreak of war had effectively stopped all plans for the rebuilding of Holloway, the need for improvements there was not forgotten. The Report of the Prison Commissioners for 1942 suggested the revision of the former system of classification and the mixing of various types of prisoners for the purpose of training schemes. This was an important departure from the widely-held theory that hardened and experienced prisoners might 'contaminate' newcomers, and the report went as far as to say that 'it was more likely that the majority of decent (women) would influence the minority for good rather than the other way round'. Small relaxations made some difference to life: library books were now virtually available to all, irrespective of the 'stage' reached, conversation at exercise was allowed and the standard of clothing issued was improved to a degree that effectively did away with the concept of a prison uniform.

The influx of detainees in Holloway under Regulation 18B came to an end, and as the prison population dropped to about 300 peacetime conditions gradually prevailed once more. Pressure for alternative premises was resumed as the war ended. The Prison Commissioners' concept of another large

Page 103 (above) Aerial view of Holloway Prison and district, 1953; (below) crowds waiting outside the Prison in 1955 for the official notice of Ruth Ellis's execution

Page 104 (*above*) The beginning of the demolition of the old Hollo-way in January 1971; (*below*) an architect's model for the design of the new prison at Holloway. The present 'centre' is on the right of what will be the prison campus, and the tall buildings in the top right-hand corner of the model represent the staff living-quarters outside the prison perimeter.

prison on modern lines to replace Holloway had been revised, new thinking now favouring a series of smaller prisons, each with a capacity of about 100, to be built in various parts of the country near to large towns. This would allow greater scope for attracting staff and thus provide more individual attention to prisoners, and would also be more convenient for visitors, for prisoners would, where possible, be lodged in the prison nearest to their homes. Holloway was not to be demolished immediately, though this would be the fate of Pentonville Prison, from where male prisoners would be transferred to Holloway until Pentonville itself was rebuilt outside London. But once again the needs of the Prison Commissioners were given low priority in the vast mass of reconstruction and development schemes which the end of the war had engendered.

Nevertheless two things showed that the Home Office was not entirely neglecting women prisoners. In 1945 Holloway saw the appointment of its first woman governor, Dr Charity Taylor, nearly half a century after it had become a women's prison. Two years later came the opening of Askham Grange, a large country house near York, as Britain's first open prison for women, with Miss Size as governor. The intention was that it should take first offenders between the ages of twenty-five and fifty, with at least six months' sentence still to serve, but being largely experimental, Askham Grange in fact took in many girls under 25 and the administration was flexible.

The Criminal Justice Act of 1948 made further changes in the treatment of women in prison. Penal servitude was officially abolished, together with hard labour, and the old system of allocating prisoners to the three divisions came to an end. A further important change at Holloway was that from 1948 women who did not wish their children to be born in prison could elect to be confined at the Royal Northern or another local hospital. They would be returned to Holloway after two or three days, and would be able to have their babies with them for nine months. If, after this time, the mother had a substantial part of her sentence still to serve, the child was removed and either cared for by relatives or placed in the care of the county in which she lived. In practice, if conditions were suitable, most mothers were transferred to one of the open prisons that gradually became established, where they were allowed to keep the child up to the age of two years.

The 1948 Act also modified the former system of corrective training. Under the new scheme a woman convicted of an offence attracting a sentence of two years or more, and who had been convicted of two indictable offences since the age of seventeen, could be sent for a period of corrective training for a period of two to four years, or more in particularly difficult cases. Two wings at Holloway had to be set aside for this new type of offender, about 100 of them arriving during the next two years.

Once again, after the first enthusiasm that accompanies most new ideas had waned, probation officers tended to recommend this course less and less. However, a hard core of about twenty such women was to be found in Holloway during the early 1950s and benefitted from the individual treatment given to them. The kind of corrective training they underwent consisted of courses in cooking, home-making, child welfare and general domestic duties, and even extended to classes in art and drama and the publication of their own magazine. This was tuition of a kind which the permanent staff of Holloway could not supply, being given by devoted volunteers outside the prison service. The result of all this was highly encouraging, and the Report of the Commissioners for 1953 says that in many cases the resentment felt at the length of the sentence 'had been replaced, in many women, by a certain pride in belonging to a category which is achieving something'.

Indeed, so successful did this form of training seem to be in prison that the Home Office decided to apply it to certain ordinary prisoners as part of their sentence, in the hope that it would exert the same beneficial effect. At first this nearly wrecked the scheme. The ordinary prisoners felt aggrieved and insulted at the suggestion that they needed the training normally reserved for recidivists incapable of running their own lives outside prison, and those on the scheme were equally resentful at their private and exclusive world being invaded by prisoners who did not really wish to undergo the training. The difficulties were to some extent resolved when certain women on the corrective-training scheme were transferred to the open prison at Askham Grange, by then under the governorship of Mrs Joanna Kelley who had replaced Miss Size on her second and final retirement in 1951.

Even so the number of women detainees under the scheme continued to drop as it became apparent that while a woman might be a model prisoner and amenable to training in prison, this often had little effect on her activities when once released. It could in fact be argued that proficiency in amateur dramatics and training in letter-writing might even increase her ability to engage in that most common of female offences, obtaining goods and money by deception, and make apprehension that much more difficult!

The population of Holloway, as the largest clearing-house of women prisoners in Britain, continued to be a very mixed one. Nearly a third of those detained were on remand awaiting trial or sentence. Those awaiting trial, and therefore still not considered guilty, created much additional work for the staff as they were not subject to many of the normal prison regulations. They could have meals sent in from outside at their own expense, were allowed visitors at all normal times, and could send and receive letters far more frequently than convicted women. This situation still applies today, and a great deal of time is wasted by prison officers who constantly have to accompany remanded prisoners to the courts and back again. Under existing law no person can be remanded in custody for more than eight days without being brought before a magistrate and a further remand requested. Magistrates usually grant this request, but if police enquiries are protracted they are likely to suggest, after three or four remands, that the defendant be allowed bail. This usually has the effect of speeding-up police action.

Because of this system and the number of women remanded to Holloway, there is a constant traffic between the prison and the courts. Even if the court concerned is 100 miles away, defendant and escort of two prison officers must make the journey there and back for proceedings which probably last less than five minutes. Staff shortage at Holloway is not improved having on any one day up to fifty officers touring the country on escort duty. A simplified system to replace this expensive and time-wasting process will have to be devised by the Home Office. It is suggested that requests for remands could be dealt with at a central court in the London area, or on the application of a solicitor at the original court and on the signature of a magistrate, without the defendant having to make a personal appearance each time. Prison officers are, of course, *not* part of the police force, but are members of the Prison Officers' Association. They are responsible for the prisoner or detainee while in custody, and while on the way to court, where the 'body' is handed over to the regular constabulary. As the catchment area of Holloway covers sixteen counties (an increase in the original 'Thirteen Counties' of Lady Carter's scheme) the amount of travelling involved is considerable.

Just over thirty years after the notorious affair of Edith Thompson, another hanging took place at Holloway. This did not arouse public interest to the same degree, probably because the woman accused was a Greek Cypriot and could speak hardly any English, and possibly because the affair took place only a year after the Christie murders of Notting Hill, on which controversy was still raging and tending to obscure less gruesome matters.

In 1937 a young Cypriot, Stavros Christofi, had come to England to seek work, and in 1942 had married an attractive German-born girl called Hella. They settled in Hampstead, eventually had three children and were a happy and united family. In July 1953 the mother of Stavros arrived from Cyprus on what was intended to be a holiday of a few weeks. She was a neurotic and difficult woman, and though she had not seen her son for several years immediately began to interfere in the running of the house, and became increasingly jealous and critical of her daughter-in-law. The situation was not improved by Hella's inability to speak Greek and Mrs Christofi's lack of English. Between the two the unfortunate Stavros was forced to keep the peace, but as he worked as an insurance agent by day and a waiter at a Soho restaurant most nights he was not altogether successful. As Mrs Christofi showed less and less inclination to return to Cyprus the situation became more tense, until at last the young husband suggested that Hella and the children went to Germany for a short holiday with his parents-in-law, immediately after which his mother would return home. This arrangement evidently played on Mrs Christofi's mind and determined her not to be separated from her grandchildren.

A few nights later, while Hella was taking a bath, the distraught woman battered her to death and, dragging the body into the garden, lit a bonfire round it in an attempt to get rid of the evidence. Inevitably the fire was seen by neighbours who, to their horror, realised that what at first sight seemed to be a tailor's dummy in the flames was in fact the body of a young woman.

At her trial at the Old Bailey she was found guilty, and it was then revealed that in Athens, thirty years before, she had been charged with the attempted murder of her own mother-in-law by ramming a lighted torch down her throat while she slept. In view of this her counsel wished to enter a plea of insanity in mitigation, to which Mrs Christofi objected most strenuously. In the event the plea was not accepted after psychiatrists and doctors had pronounced her sane and responsible for her actions. She was hanged at Holloway in October 1954. Today a woman with a similar record of violence would almost certainly be dealt with under the provisions of the 1959 Mental Health Act and detained in Broadmoor.

This was the second hanging in Holloway's history. The third and last was not far off.

Despite the outcry surrounding the execution of Edith Thompson in 1923 and the hope that this would be the last execution of a woman in Britain, this was very far from the case. Between Edith Thompson and Mrs Christofi, thirty years later, sixty-six women in Britain had been condemned to death, though only nine of them had actually been executed. The tragic case of Ruth Ellis, who achieved the distinction of being the last woman to be hanged in Britain, came only a year after the Christofi case.

At the end of the war Ruth Ellis was only eighteen, but was already married and divorced. She became manageress of a drinking-club in Kensington and by 1953 was living with David Blakely, a racing-driver three years her junior. In April 1955 she suffered a miscarriage, and Blakely, who had long been showing evidence of tiring of her, decided to move out. Ruth Ellis's world began to crumble. After repeated attempts to persuade him to return to her she finally decided that if she could not have him, then nobody else would. Accordingly, one Sunday evening, she followed him to a pub in Hampstead where he was drinking with friends, waited until he came out, and calmly shot him dead. She made no attempt to escape and when asked why she had shot him gave what was for her the only logical explanation: 'Because I wanted to kill him.'

She was tried and sentenced to death. In Holloway she refused to allow an appeal to be lodged, but the few friends who rallied round her at length persuaded her to agree to a petition for her reprieve to be forwarded to the Home Secretary. It was of no avail. During her last days in Holloway's condemned cell she displayed a stoicism that moved the prison officers in charge of her to describe her as the bravest woman they had ever met. She was hanged in the prison on 13 July 1955, while a large crowd assembled outside to watch the customary notice of execution being posted on the gate.

She was twenty-eight years of age, as was Edith Thompson, and once again rumours of gruesome scenes at her execution began to circulate, fanned by the somewhat unnecessary publication of the comment by the prison doctor that on conducting the post-mortem he noticed a smell of alcohol on her lips. And why not, indeed? If the last request of Ruth Ellis in this world had been for a double-Scotch to ease her passage into eternity, was it likely to have been refused?

In 1964 Sidney Silverman, MP, moved the Murder (Abolition of the Death Penalty) Bill which was subsequently adopted, and Ruth Ellis took her place in penal history as almost certainly the last woman to be hanged in Britain. According to custom she was buried in the prison grounds in an unmarked grave, the location of which was known only to the governor and to the Home Office. In 1970, when preparations were made to demolish and rebuild Holloway, her relations were given the opportunity of having her body reburied elsewhere. Her remains were removed, and immediately the news became known some residents of the town concerned raised an outcry. The efforts of those who tried to ban the reinterment failed, and today Ruth Ellis lies in peace in the beech-clad slopes of the Chiltern Hills.

The last years of the old Holloway have been a period of comparative calm within, but with much discussion and study of its problems by organisations outside. In 1959 Mrs Joanna Kelley, who had been in charge of Askham Grange, came to Holloway as governor and remained until 1966 when she was appointed Assistant Director of Prisons and as such responsible for all female penitentiaries in Britain. Her place at Holloway was taken by Mrs Dorothy Wing.

In her book *When the Gates Shut* (1967), Mrs Kelley described in vivid detail many of the problems that arose at Holloway during her period of office affecting both prisoners and staff, and much of the material that follows is drawn from this source. Like most people concerned with prisons and their function, Mrs Kelley did not give up hope of one day seeing Holloway replaced by a more suitable building. From time to time various suggestions had been made, including the transfer of Holloway prisoners to a new prison at Theydon Bois, Essex, but had come to nothing. But though the fate of Holloway remained undecided, progress was being made in the provision of other types of penal establishments elsewhere in the country: a semi-secure prison for young offenders and 'corrective trainees' was opened at Styal, Manchester, which later accommodated Borstal girls and their babies. With additional Borstal establishments at Bullwood Hall, Essex and East Sutton Park, Kent, the population of Holloway had been reduced and those still in custody there now represented rather less than half of all women prisoners in Britain.

In 1966, the year that Mrs Kelley became Assistant Director of Prisons, the government set up an Advisory Council on the Penal System under the chairmanship of Mr Kenneth Younger. Two years later, as a result of the Council's report, the government published its findings and suggestions on several aspects of the penal system including the future of Holloway. This was that, as no other suitable site could be found within easy access of the London courts, the existing prison should be demolished and a new one erected on the site. In July 1968 the Holloway Project Group was formed and the arduous task of planning began. In 1970, after it had been in constant use for nearly 120 years, Holloway began to be demolished and rebuilt in a project originally scheduled for completion in 1977 and at an estimated cost of £6 million. At the time of writing escalating costs coupled with shortage of materials makes it unlikely that the estimate will be contained at that figure, or that the new Holloway will be completed before 1980.

In 1972 Mrs Wing retired and her place as governor was taken by Dr Mary Bull, a physician and psychiatrist who for some time had been a member of the medical staff of the prison.

8

WOMEN OFFENDERS TODAY AND THEIR TREATMENT

During this century the number of women sent to prison annually in Britain has shown a remarkable decrease. 49,000 women were sentenced to prison in 1899, but by 1913 this had reduced to 34,000. In 1921 the figure was 11,000 and by 1960 had dropped to 2,000. In 1972 about 1,000 women were sentenced to immediate prison or Borstal, and about 2,000 given suspended sentences under the provisions of the 1972 Criminal Justice Act.

Although the numbers seem to have settled, with just under 1,000 women being in prison at any one time compared with about 37,000 men, it is the rise of juvenile female delinquency that is worrying the authorities. Not only is the non-violent nature of female criminality changing, but violence is now being demonstrated by a far younger age-group. Reports have been issued showing that offences by girls between the ages of fourteen and seventeen increased to about 2,000 during 1972, and in that same year over 40 per cent of all the burglaries in Birmingham were committed by girls in that age-group. (*The Guardian*, 30 July 1973.)

Various theories have been propounded to account for this state of affairs. One group of lawyers investigating the problem

thinks it may be the result of the application of the 1969
Children & Young Persons Act, which removed from juvenile
courts the power to send young people to hostels and
handed over control of children to the social services. As social
workers may be more fully trained in the *theories* of juvenile
delinquency, but less experienced at dealing with offenders in
practice, they are, perhaps, more gullible than magistrates
and readier to allow the child to return home when suitable
accommodation is hard to find. The superintendent of the
Cumberlow Remand Home in South London, on the other
hand, thinks the trouble springs from the sudden transition
of girls from small primary schools to the less restricted and
supervised secondary modern schools, where to assert their
personality they may feel they must indulge in aggressive
behaviour. But one point this particular observer has made is
that aggressive and nonconformist behaviour is by no means
limited to girls of low intelligence or from 'broken' or even
unhappy homes. Only too often it is the child who is given
everything she asks for at home, and where restrictions are
minimal, who causes trouble later when she finds she has to
conform to regulations.

Sociologists point out that a rise in female delinquency often
goes hand-in-hand with the increased emancipation of women,
and remind us that the last outbreak of this kind coincided with
the war years, when women were employed on war work and
their children evacuated. Yet another aspect of the situation is
the increase in the number of West Indian women in Britain.
This is not to say that these women are more prone to crime,
but that in an argument they are more accustomed to settling
the matter by physical means rather than with the verbal abuse
that is the normal weapon of the Englishwoman.

Whatever the cause (and the above are only a few of the many
put forward), the increase of crimes of violence by women is
16.6 per cent, as against an increase of 11.8 per cent in male
offenders. Equally unsatisfactory is the increase in non-violent

activities such as larceny and false pretences, where the rise is 10.2 per cent for women and only 5.9 per cent for men. *The Police Review* commented on these figures in 1972: 'Mothers and wives who are becoming increasingly delinquent will almost certainly fail to imbue a moral sense in their families or act as a restraining influence.'

Yet despite these gloomy forebodings, figures published in a White Paper in December 1973 show a reduction in the total number of offenders of both sexes at present in prison, Borstal or detention centres, from 39,708 to 38,328, representing a drop of 3.5 per cent in twelve months. Of the latter figure, 980 were women. To the sociologist this may be encouraging, but to those concerned with penal reform it is still worrying that at present nearly half these women are in prison in Holloway. This has not created problems in overcrowding (for Holloway, it will be remembered, was built to accommodate 500), but rather in the segregation of various classes of detainees. These fall into the following categories.

1. Women serving sentences, sub-divided into (a) first-offenders and (b) recidivists
2. Women on remand awaiting trial or sentence
3. Borstal recalls
4. Young girls considered 'unruly' under the Act.

These categories, together with further sub-divisions (as, for example, the domestic-training section for those sentenced for child neglect, and one wing used entirely as a hospital), create a complicated pattern of administration and security.

First offenders ('Star' prisoners) are separated from the others as far as possible. Recidivists (habitual offenders) are no longer sub-divided according to the length of sentence, which is one simplification, but in fact continue to be the most troublesome kind of inmate. Many Holloway recidivists are elderly habitual drunkards. For them Holloway is a home-from-home, where they are so familiar with the routine that they will complain bitterly if their usual cell is not available. Some even insist on being issued with the long-discarded grey prison cap, and a small number of these are kept in stock to oblige the 'regulars'.

The problem of the habitual drunkard has never been successfully solved at Holloway since the first attempts to 'convert' them by sending them to the Inebriate Reformatory at Aylesbury were made at the turn of the century. Most people believe that prison is not the right place for such women, and through the years many treatments and experiments have been tried, most of them valueless but all accepted with a cheerful scepticism by the women concerned. Drunkenness as a whole has decreased during this century, but there is still a hard core of regular alcoholics who know only too well that whatever befalls there will always be a light in the window for them in their fairy castle near the Nag's Head, N7.

Offences connected with prostitution have also changed their pattern during the last fifteen years, particularly the offence of soliciting. From 1840 until the passing of the Street Offences Act of 1959, the fine for soliciting had been a maximum of £2. For the average prostitute this amount was only a tiny percentage of her earnings, looked upon as virtually the cost of a licence to continue her calling.

In 1954 the Wolfenden Committee was set up to examine this and other problems (including homosexuality), and recommended that the penalty for soliciting should be increased to a maximum fine of £25 and three months' imprisonment. This was adopted, though not without a certain amount of opposition from those who saw in it the standard British expedient of curing a situation by 'brushing it under the carpet' so it appeared no longer to exist. In fact this is what happened, though for the first year after the Act was passed the result was a sudden influx of prostitutes into Holloway. But later the pattern changed, as girls 'on the game' no longer thronged the streets of Soho and London's West End but went under cover, working from pubs and clubs, soliciting from cars, and making it almost impossible for the police to control their activities.

In fact, as experience in other countries has shown, it is extremely difficult for the law to deal with this problem. Until the last war about nineteen countries had a system of licensed brothels, including France and Italy. In Paris 2,000 girls were working in 'maisons tolerées', with ten times that number operating freelance outside the law. When licensed brothels were closed in 1946 and replaced by a licence system involving a card which guaranteed freedom from infection, the prostitute population of Paris was still about 20,000, with only 6,000 carrying cards and the rest working illegally.

Italy, which banned state brothels in 1958, found that the incidence of syphilis increased immediately as a result of freelance workers on the streets, and by 1960 twice as many people were infected as had been before brothels were closed. In Britain state-licensed brothels were discontinued as far back as 1751 and there has been little demand for their reopening, though the Wolfenden Committee was not naïve enough to expect that its recommendations would have much effect on prostitution as a whole.

The reason why girls go 'on the game' has been the subject of many solemn enquiries by sociologists and others, and has resulted in a great deal of nonsense being talked. So-called 'broken homes' are often a contributory factor, as may be a traumatic sexual experience, such as rape or incest, suffered by a girl when very young. But basically the reason why most girls become prostitutes is for no more complex reason than to earn money—and to earn it at ten or twenty times the rate offered by more conventional work. Despite the belief held by many innocent social workers, girls are rarely 'snared' by a professional ponce. Once they have embarked on their career, usually as 'keen amateurs', and discovered how much they can earn, they themselves look round for a ponce to go into partnership with, coming to a suitable arrangement as regards commission. Most prostitutes pay this commission willingly in return for the respectability a regular male companion can provide, and also for the security against attacks by perverts, which is one of the occupational hazards of 'the game'. The prostitute regulates her hours of work as strictly as does the secretary or factory-worker, with definite days off in company with the ponce, or perhaps visiting her child away at boarding-school. She may well marry, eventually, and in such cases often assumes a degree of respectability and standards far higher than that of her neighbours.

After a prostitute has been on the game for a short time she ceases to gain any pleasure from the sex act, and indeed may never have had any pleasure from it from the beginning. It is purely a job of work. The prostitute who goes through the pockets of her sleeping or befuddled companion and steals his money has been the subject of a recent pronouncement by a psychiatrist, who put forward the view that this is a phenomenon induced by a desire to humiliate men and to deprive them of every vestige of their masculinity—the so-called 'castration syndrome'. In fact the only 'syndrome' present is the desire for more money, the motive being no more concerned with castration than that behind any other form of theft.

During World War II many prostitutes in London were used unofficially by the Intelligence Service to gather information on suspect aliens and others, for it is well known that a man will confide in a prostitute far more freely than he will with other casual acquaintances. Those members of Intelligence who had to employ these girls were constantly impressed by their efficiency, loyalty and devotion to duty ('I look on this as my war-work, dear!') and found that a valuable and un-emotional relationship, with useful advantages to the security of the state, could be established. Occasionally the difficulty was to avoid too close a liaison with the girl concerned and to keep the situation at a business level ('Stay the night, dear—I never charge my friends'), but most girls realised that the operative had a job of work to do. In fact the Intelligence men found it was far more difficult to achieve this kind of withdrawal tactfully, without giving offence, than to resist the temptation to stay, which was usually minimal.

There was a strict convention that a prostitute who happened to meet an Intelligence operative unexpectedly would never show the slightest sign of recognition.

In prison the prostitute can be a source of difficulty through her strong resentment against the very fact that she has been sentenced. She feels she is supplying a need that has existed since mankind began, and sees no reason for the law to impose moral sanctions on her. Another complication, frequently found in Holloway, is that because the prostitute has only a physical relationship with a man, and rarely an emotional one, her emotional outlet is likely to be released by a mild form of lesbianism once she is in the sole company of other women. Some of the inmates may be disturbed and revolted by this, and trouble results. On the other hand many an otherwise normal woman discovers, in prison, a latent lesbianism which can be a source of worry, though it usually disappears once she is released.

Not that lesbianism in prison is of a very physical or sexual nature. Normally it manifests itself merely as one woman developing a 'crush' for another, with prisoners trying always to sit next to each other in chapel or in association, holding hands and passing to and fro endearing notes known in prison as 'kites'. Such emotional relationships developing in prison are considered the norm and are certainly not accorded the 'unhealthy' overtones of true lesbianism as it exists outside prison, and which newspapers would have us believe is so rife inside.

Very rarely a relationship develops between a prisoner and a prison officer. This is something which is taken very seriously, for it militates against discipline and becomes a potential source of blackmail. If such a situation arises the officer is transferred elsewhere. Occasionally difficulties can arise if a prison officer forms an attachment to a prisoner who seems truly penitent, and whom the officer thinks she can assist by private efforts in rehabilitation in prison. A rare example of this was highly publicised in 1974 when a Holloway prison officer, who had formerly been a nun, became involved with a life-serving prisoner to the extent of actively participating in a plan to escape from the prison as a prelude to the pair starting life afresh as missionaries in South America. In this instance the plot was discovered, the prisoner had a year added to her life-sentence (which meant very little) while the wretched officer was herself sentenced to a lengthy term of imprisonment.

The largest proportion of women in Holloway are those sentenced for offences connected with theft, larceny or false pretences. Most are not there because they are fundamentally 'bad', more often they are simply poor managers. Mrs Joanna Kelley commented that many of the women who come to Holloway have had little experience of living according to a budget, or of the elementary principles of running a home. All is well while the husband is in a steady job and the family fare can be provided by constant fish-and-chips or out of tins. But should the husband be put on short time or lose his job, there is an immediate crisis. The wife cannot cope with her reduced income, and for the sake of the children will resort to pilfering from shops and supermarkets to make ends meet. Overwork and illness may also be contributory factors, resulting in apathy and a disinclination to attend to household chores, which once again eventually results in problems and recourse to stealing, or to obtaining money by false pretences.

A different type is the compulsive liar, a regular inmate of Holloway with, in most cases, little prospect of being able to mend her ways. So entrenched can this habit become that it frequently persists even in prison, and Mrs Kelley tells of one such woman who successfully 'conned' her fellow-prisoners into believing that she was extremely well-connected, with friends in the South of France who would provide a holiday there, with all expenses paid, for those who had treated her well in prison. On this pretext she managed to acquire the weekly purchases of sweets and cigarettes from several girls who believed her story which, needless to say, was proved subsequently to be an entire fabrication.

There are always, in Holloway, a few abortionists, mostly professionals but also amateurs who have embarked on the trade usually for financial gain, after having had a successful abortion performed on themselves. Due to recent changes in the laws governing abortions there is likely to be a reduction in this type of prisoner.

Other inmates include women who have ill-treated their children, often one particular child being singled out for this, the mother being devoted to the others. This can be the result of the child not being wanted and therefore representing an additional and, to the mother, unnecessary tax on her time and financial resources; the ill-treatment is an expression of spite more towards the father than to the child itself.

Looking at a cross-section of women in Holloway at any given time, it becomes apparent that it is too often circumstances that have brought them there, plus an indefinable lack of character that has allowed them to succumb to the easy way out. Such hard circumstances, and lack of training in combating them, are most often found in the poorer groups of the population. While it is easy to say that this is the fault of the present social system and the inequalities it produces, obviously some action has to be taken towards women who are making themselves a nuisance. Few thinking people really believe that prison is the solution to the problem, but in the absence of any other type of penal system, those in charge of prisons have to do the best they can to help to rehabilitate the woman who transgresses the law. One cannot do away with prisons overnight. Nor is it always wise to let the prisoner know what the experts consider to be the main reason for delinquency. Those who are concerned with the administration of justice in the courts are well aware of the persistent offender who, on learning the results of a psychiatric report, begins to believe that he or she 'cannot help' being predisposed to crime. Violence on television is also used as a pretext for aggressive behaviour, for young delinquents know of the expert discussions that take place on this subject. 'What shall I say to the judge?' a girl who had pleaded guilty to robbing a post-office was heard to ask a fellow-prisoner. 'Tell him it's the violence on telly', was the answer. 'He'll give the court a lecture for twenty minutes about it, and then let you off light because you've proved his point.'

The delinquent young, though notoriously preoccupied with their own affairs apparently to the total exclusion of everything else, are capable of devising highly ingenious methods of avoiding the consequences of their actions. For this reason many magistrates, particularly those with long years of experience, sometimes become a little cynical when listening to the so-called 'mitigating circumstances' that have caused a girl or woman to run foul of the law. For the defendant it may be a novel and ingenious excuse. Too often, for the magistrate, it is something he has heard many times before. It is only the presence of a social or welfare report corroborating the evidence that is likely to affect the sentence or treatment prescribed.

With the varying attitudes to crime found amongst those who are sentenced, it is an encouraging sign that courts are tending to rely more and more on medical and psychiatric reports before deciding on the disposal of those who come before them. This applies particularly to women, for only with the greatest reluctance does a magistrate send a woman to prison. She may well be remanded to Holloway while a report is being prepared, but though in custody is not subject to the same restrictions as those already sentenced.

The compilation of reports of various kinds takes up a great deal of time of the medical staff at Holloway. Two or three weeks are normally allowed for a report, which can include three kinds of psychological test. If the girl has a previous criminal history, reports may have to be obtained from probation officers or from those who have had dealings with her in the past. A combined report is finally returned to the court concerned, which assesses the best course of action to take. It may be Borstal, a prison sentence in Holloway or in an open prison such as Askham Grange, or a suspended sentence. It could equally well be probation, subject to agreement to undertake certain training or treatment. In very serious cases, such as child murder, the provisions of the 1959 Mental Health Act may be invoked.

It sometimes happens that a woman finds herself mentally disturbed as the result of having a child, or at her inability to have a child, and can cause injury or even death either to her own infant or to that of another woman. Where the courts think fit as a result of the psychiatrist's report, such a woman would not stand trial at the Crown Court, but be sent to Broadmoor or Rampton or to one of the two other 'special hospitals' in England designated by the Act. These, it should be stressed, are not prisons, but come under the jurisdiction of the Ministry of Health & Social Security. Nevertheless, the Home Office has the final word, both under Sections 72 and 65 of the Mental Health Act, on the decision to send a woman there and on her release, possibly many years later.

The medical care of those in Holloway is of a high order, and most women improve considerably in health while there. Once the first shock of being in prison is over, most women benefit from the regular hours and meals and the right amount of sleep. Illnesses normally considered to be caused by stress, such as gastric ulcers and hypertension, are rare, and there is also a curious resistance to epidemics of various kinds—a feature of life in Holloway which has existed since Victorian times.

Prisoners also have the advantage over those outside the walls in being able to see a doctor daily on request. Those serving long sentences are given a routine examination monthly. Many girls ask to have tattoo-marks removed, and become extremely self-conscious about the social stigma that this form of decoration is supposed to represent.

Dentists, opticians, chiropodists and physiotherapists all visit the prison at regular intervals and about 600 women annually are treated at local hospitals as out-patients when the prison hospital cannot provide the specialist treatment required.

The psychotherapist probably has the most difficult task in the treatment and rehabilitation of prisoners. To some women life in prison represents what seems the ideal situation—a total dependence on others and no necessity to organise anything. To inculcate into this type of woman, who once again is really a poor manager and a social misfit, rather than a mental case, a desire to use her own initiative and assume responsibilities, is almost impossible under a regime that takes over and organises almost every moment of her day and does not encourage free expression. With other women the difficulty is the reverse—it is exactly this stifling and organised existence, which the prisoner immediately wants to reject, that makes rehabilitation such a problem.

At one time the work given to prisoners was intended to provide punishment in a form that was arduous, meaningless and largely non-productive. Today it is the accepted view that offenders are sent to prison *as* punishment and not *for* punishment. As was demonstrated earlier, the idea that the work must be useless soon became outdated and even the treadmill was used to provide energy for machinery.

But there are many other reasons why work of a useful kind should be provided in prisons. Apart from the relief of boredom, there is also the therapeutic effect of the satisfaction engendered by creative enterprise, however elementary this may be. There is also the fact that the work can provide some form of vocational training for the outside world. Yet another factor is that the prison population represents a considerable labour force that should not be wasted.

In Holloway, as elsewhere, work is used to a great extent as a form of rehabilitation. But not all women want to work, and the system which allows prisoners to see the doctor when they desire it, to seek interviews with the governor or (for those who are appealing against sentence) to spend time in writing letters concerning their case, makes it possible for a determined woman to avoid nearly all work if she gives her mind to it. This itself, it could be argued, is not always a bad thing if it causes someone to use her initiative; but this type of prisoner is too often in prison in the first place as a result of having excess, or ill-directed, initiative or imagination.

But for those willing to co-operate there is a variety of tasks, from scrubbing and cleaning to vocational courses requiring a high degree of concentration and aptitude. Some women work in the laundry and in the kitchens, others in Holloway's famous jam factory, some taking a real pride in the results of their labour. Probably the most hardworking and most conscientious women are those employed in Reception, who remember all too clearly their own first shattering experience of prison life; their sympathetic attitude to new arrivals does much to reduce the initial shock. A number of women work in the prison workshops on complicated machinery manufacturing garments such as dungarees and uniforms. Less able women are given tuition in the manufacture of soft toys and simpler objects.

Unfortunately the adequate supervision of a large number of women doing a full day's work requires a shift system not possible with the number of prison officers available. On the whole, throughout the prison system, both male and female, there is therefore insufficient work available and most prisoners spend far too much time alone in their cells. In any case, because payment for work is on a 'pocket-money' basis, there is no real incentive to work hard. Work is therefore often done in an apathetic and desultory manner, and even the simplest activity, such as cutting stamps off envelopes, is often made valueless—for example, believe it or not, by spoiling the stamps by cutting across them instead of round them.

With most forms of vocational training the problem is that most women are not in Holloway long enough for the results to be worthwhile. A particular kind of training for those serving sentences for neglect of children, inaugurated in Holloway in 1962, has in fact enjoyed some success: this is the tuition given in child welfare and domestic duties, and of those who have undertaken it less than 2 per cent have been subsequently convicted for similar offences.

The hostel that formerly existed near the prison to provide facilities for outside work for long-term prisoners nearing the end of their sentences has now been closed and transferred to Askham Grange in Yorkshire. One reason for this was that the prospects for finding suitable employment for released women were higher in York than in London. A secondary reason was that women with homes in London often tried to visit them while going to work or returning from it, often doing housework at home and overtaxing their strength, as well as finding added frustration in having to leave home and return to the prison hostel at night. The Holloway hostel, which in its final form was open for three years, was used mainly for the training and rehabilitation of recidivists, and in this context the fact that about one-third of the women passing through have not been in further trouble since release seems encouraging.

EDUCATION

The kind of vocational training outlined above stands midway between work and education, a combination of both. Formal education at Holloway is provided by a staff of outside teachers who come daily to supervise a variety of courses. These include English literature, drama, appreciation of music, current affairs and the law, as well as less academic subjects such as first-aid, dressmaking, needlework, poise and personality and basketry. Weaving and tapestry are two very popular classes, in which work can also be undertaken for sale to outside shops and stores.

Television plays an important part in the rehabilitation of women while in Holloway, giving them a sense of association with the outside world. Since 1960 the prison library has been part of the National Central Library Service and has a stock of over 12,000 books which are being constantly changed. Inmates can exchange books during the lunch-hour and can borrow as many as they like. Staff from the Borough of Camden Library frequently attend to advise prisoners on the choice of books and to deal with orders for books not in stock. Library books are a great solace to the woman who must spend many hours in her cell, and large picture-books are available to those who cannot read. As in the outside world, those who are illiterate often do not wish to admit it, and the librarian (a senior prison officer) must watch to discover those who are obviously unable to understand titles. A watch must also be kept for mutilated books, and each prisoner must sign separately for each book she borrows. The fly-leaves and any blank pages at the beginning and end of each book are numbered in order to discourage anyone tearing out the pages for use as writing-paper. (In the days before cosmetics were allowed the red covers of books were often soaked in water to provide rouge and lipstick.)

As well as borrowing books, prisoners are allowed to order their own daily newspapers and pay for them, as well as local papers and weekly and monthly magazines, most of which are sent in by relatives. At one time a strict censorship of the contents of daily papers was imposed, and any account of court proceedings relative to any prisoner was cut out of the paper or made illegible by a black ink roller. Under Mrs Kelley this practice ceased, and now the prisoners can read accounts of court cases with freedom. The result of this relaxation was unexpected: several girls of a domineering type who had formerly bullied others became much less threatening in their behaviour. They had been intimidating the others by stories of daring escapades involving attacking the police and other 'heroic' behaviour. Once their cases were read in the press many of them were found to be serving sentences for petty theft and trickery.

Newspaper and television series on prisons or courts are greeted with the greatest interest. In 1974 a television series dealing with life in a women's prison even reconstructed the only escape ever accomplished by a woman from Holloway— that of 'Blonde Mickey' who went over the wall, literally, in 1960 and made Holloway history. Three months later she was caught on the South Coast and was returned to Holloway, where a further eighteen months was added to her sentence. On her release after four years she decided to give up her former life as 'queen of the underworld', sold her life-story to a Sunday paper for a large amount and subsequently went straight.

Film shows are provided once a month in Holloway, and on most Sundays there is a concert in the prison chapel which is adapted for the purpose. Holloway seems fortunate in the attitude of its chaplain, for still today in at least one provincial prison even the dividing-off of the room for use for secular purposes is considered a sacrilege and strictly forbidden. In this same all-male prison a large amount of money has recently been spent on the provision of a magnificent pipe-organ for the chapel, an expense resented by staff and inmates alike, all feeling that the money could have been put to better use in improving other facilities around the prison.

Holloway, as has been seen, has had a tradition of education from the beginning. One of the difficulties is in assessing just what form the education of a prisoner should take, and mistakes can be made when women and girls are reluctant to say in just what they consider themselves deficient. It is not very much use giving a girl a course in current affairs or world history when it is discovered, as happened on one occasion,

129

that what she really wants to know, but has never dared ask, is how to behave at table and what the various kinds of cutlery are for.

Until 1921 attendance at religious services in prison was compulsory except for those of the Roman Catholic faith, whose religion forbade them to attend services of another denomination. Since 1961 the regulations have been changed, and while the Prison Department lays down that every woman in Holloway shall have the right to worship in her own particular faith, this is no longer obligatory. But a prisoner must still ask for permission to miss divine service, and most find it easier to conform than not.

At one time the chapel at Holloway was interdenominational, but in 1936 an outbuilding was 'converted' into a Roman Catholic church which existed until the reconstruction of this part of the prison in 1973.

Discovering a prisoner's true religious affinities (if she has any) on entering Holloway is not an easy matter and, as happens in the services, any hesitation in answering such a question is likely to be translated into 'C of E'. In fact a high proportion of Holloway inmates have no strong religious feelings when admitted. The comparatively high number of those professing to be Roman Catholics (as many as 35 per cent according to a recent survey) must be considered suspect for, again as in the services, many people think they will gain some advantage or preferential treatment by this means.

Many people outside prison have a cynical attitude to 'prison religion'. Whilst it is true that many women attend services as a means of escape from the crushing boredom of prison life, for others the very act of going to church and taking part in a service is a genuinely new and exciting experience. Many have never spoken to a minister of religion in their lives, and are pleasantly surprised at the attitude shown to them.

Every new arrival in Holloway is interviewed by the chaplain who must try and assess the personality and problems of the prisoner in a short space of time without appearing to be unduly inquisitive. The chaplain also sees all women immediately prior to release. In between the Sunday morning service (there is no evening service) and the Wednesday mid-week afternoon service he may visit women in their cells. As an almost anonymous figure, neither one of 'us' nor one of 'them', he can provide an opportunity for a woman to relieve her tensions simply by listening while she pours out her troubles.

There is a Bible-reading class, and an important and successful experiment at Holloway was the introduction of a weekly 'quiet time' lasting about three hours. The women in the group, usually twenty or thirty, place themselves under a rule of silence, the chaplain or a visiting clergyman reads a lesson or two, tea is taken in silence and the period ends with Evensong in the chapel. Full-length religious retreats lasting a week or a fortnight have been conducted from time to time, particularly for Roman Catholics, to whom this is an established part of their faith.

Just how much effect 'prison religion' has on a wrongdoer is difficult to gauge. As Mrs Kelley has pointed out, people go to prison not because they are intrinsically wicked but because they have broken the law, which means they have offended against current ethics and morality. Many of the women serving sentences in Holloway have standards of morals peculiarly their own. The present spate of shoplifting is due very largely to a moral code which believes that whilst it *may* be wrong to steal from a private individual or small shopkeeper, the wholesale pilfering of goods from a departmental store is harmless.

At best religious instruction in prison may cause a woman to 'repent of her ways' and decide to try and lead a better life in future. At the very least it may help to ease the bitterness and frustration engendered by a prison sentence, and may help her

131

to come to terms with herself and with her fellow-prisoners. Perhaps it is not too much to hope that this will have a beneficial effect on her attitude to life when she is once more free.

Most women who have written about their experiences in Holloway have commented that the most soul-destroying aspect of the system is the anonymity that pervades the atmosphere, and the complete loss of individuality. It is a long time since women prison officers were forbidden to look at an inmate whilst issuing instructions, or to give any sign at all of personal involvement with them. The situation has now moved very much the other way, and, as will be shown when the provisions for the New Holloway are discussed, the impersonality of prison life will soon be a thing of the past. In the meantime there are always a certain number of women who never wish to mix, and who give the impression that they fear contamination from associating with others in prison. For these the enforced 'togetherness' that the New Holloway is likely to impose will be almost as traumatic an experience as is solitary confinement for the average inmate under present conditions.

9

THE PRISON OFFICER

Seven years after Holloway became an all-women's prison, Lady Constance Lytton, one of the most articulate and influential of the suffragettes, sister of the Earl of Lytton, spent some time there. On the occasion of her first arrest her identity was known, and she was given preferential treatment. But on the second occasion she had purposely dressed as a working woman and gave a false name. Her treatment was very different indeed and led to hardships which resulted in her being a semi-invalid for the rest of her life.

On her release she wrote several articles for the press on conditions in Holloway which were later to have a profound effect on the treatment of women offenders. In particular she criticised the demeanour of the wardresses who, as mentioned in the last chapter and presumably on Home Office instructions, habitually addressed prisoners in flat, monotonous tones, with no inflexion of the voice, carefully looking away as they spoke and never addressing them directly. Presumably the idea was to create in the offender a feeling of anonymity and complete depersonalisation, and, if Lady Constance is to be believed, it succeeded. The prisoner was treated as less than human, but the wardress, in implementing this policy, was herself reduced to the role of a cell-locking automaton and severely discouraged from taking any interest in her charges.

Today most officers in all prisons take a keen interest in the welfare of those under their care and the rehabilitation of the offender is very largely due to the relationship with prison staff that develops. This is an integral part of the training that all prison officers now receive at Wakefield before being allocated to a prison. At the prison a further twelve-month probationary period is served before trainees become established prison officers.

Prison officers are not part of the police force in Britain, and it was not until 1939 that their own union was recognised. But the early history of the struggle for recognition is closely bound up with the efforts of the police for the same right, a struggle which came into the open in the last months of the 1914-18 War. At midnight on Friday 30 August 1918, the entire Metropolitan Police Force came out on strike. The following day, Saturday, they marched *en masse* to Downing Street, to the bewilderment of the rest of Britain and to the panic of the government. They marched under the banner of the National Union of Police & Prison Officers (NUPPO) led by their chairman, Constable James Marston, and the Honorary Secretary, John Crisp, and were met at Downing Street by Lloyd George, the Prime Minister, and other members of the Cabinet. Within half an hour, Marston and Crisp were able to announce that recognition of the union had been granted.

The Prime Minister had suggested that recognition would be given when the war was over, but that in the meantime Representative Boards should be set-up, consisting of police and Home Office officials, to look into complaints of working conditions in the police force and prisons. When in November 1918 the war came to a sudden and unexpected end, the Police Union began to make plans for the final realisation of its hopes for full recognition by the Home Office. However, it soon became apparent that Lloyd George had no intention of giving way as easily as it had appeared, and the Representative Boards were obviously intended to take the place of the union and to continue indefinitely. The result was another Metropolitan police strike in London in 1919, but this time the war was over and less pressure could be brought to bear on a government which, a year before, had appeared to agree to anything to get the police back to work—haunted by the Russian revolution then only ten months old. Lloyd George was to say later that the only reason he acquiesced to police demands in 1918 was because at that moment Britain stood nearer to Bolshevism than at any time since.

This time enthusiasm for the strike was lukewarm, even in the force itself, and the City of London Police refused to come out, as did many forces in the provinces. The government acted swiftly. In October 1919 the Police Act was rushed through Parliament making it illegal for any member of the force to withdraw his labour. Though not specifically mentioned in the act those in the prison service were also effectively stopped from striking or even forming their own association, and seventy warders from Wormwood Scrubs who had come out with the police were dismissed immediately. The Representative Boards remained, one early change being the substitution of the word 'prison officer' for 'warder'. This was a change that cost little.

What might have cost money, and were therefore ignored, were the deplorable conditions under which prison officers worked. The Representative Boards were financed and almost entirely controlled by the Home Office, and all decisions of the Boards were final and allowed of no appeal.

It is not surprising that, under these circumstances, resentment smouldered and recruitment to the prison service dropped almost to nothing. From time to time the Home Office, under various Home Secretaries, expressed its intention of embarking on a programme of prison reform, but it was plain that reform, in this context, meant reform of conditions for prisoners rather than for staff. There were then, and have always been since, a large number of well-intentioned people deeply concerned with the welfare and rehabilitation of prisoners but with no thought for those who have most to do with them—the prison officers. The officers had no union nor any association to speak for them, and unbelievable as this may seem, this state of affairs continued during most of the period between the two World Wars.

In 1936, after several secret and potentially dangerous meetings between the Civil Servants Clerical Association (the official civil-service union) and prison officers, the latter won their point and became affiliated to the Police Federation. This was still unsatisfactory, though certainly a step forward, for the conditions of work and duties involved in the prison service were not comparable with conditions in the police force. It was not until 1939 that the Prison Officers' Association was at last officially formed, twenty years after the ban on such an organisation had first been imposed.

Today the Association has a total membership of over 14,000 and represents 98 per cent of those who are qualified to join. This is probably a higher percentage of membership than is found in any other union not operating a 'closed shop' policy.

Women members of the Prison Officers' Association number about 800 in England and Wales, but this includes nearly 400 who do not work in prisons but in the three 'special hospitals' of Broadmoor, Rampton and Moss Side, which house those once termed the 'criminally insane'. Of the remaining 400 women, about 150 are at Holloway, of whom about 100 are concerned purely with disciplinary matters.

Today's prison officer at Holloway is no longer an intimidating gaoler. Wearing a smart blue two-piece suit with white blouse open at the neck, she is not frightening to talk to, and many women in Holloway for the first time have come to trust the prison officer as a friend in whom they can confide.

Whatever wing a girl is in at Holloway a prison officer is never very far away. The prison's famous 'centre' is not only the geographical centre of Holloway from which all the cell-blocks radiate but also the focus of a complex administrative organisation. Round this lofty hall the day-to-day life of the prison revolves. Here prison officers sign on and off duty, depositing and collecting their keys and making a note of the special instructions posted on the board before their tour of duty. There is a constant flow of traffic through the centre to and from the wings with much locking and unlocking of doors, for since 1960 the ends of the wings have been blocked off so that the centre has become a large octagonal space with doors leading through to the wings and to other parts of the prison. Each wing has thus become a self-contained unit and is no longer visible from the centre.

Flanking the main entrance to this area are two glass-fronted booths, occupied by two senior officers, who constantly supervise activities, control the issue of keys, pass on messages and issue instructions. The original spiral staircase of iron still contributes its own noisy quota as women pass up and down in what seems a never-ending stream. In the middle of the centre a low table holds a permanent display of flowers and at the bottom of the stairs hangs a handsome brass bell originally from Newgate. Nearby the prison cat, the latest of a long line of mousers always called 'Dinkie', snoozes contentedly during the day, sublimely oblivious of the constant bustle and noise that seems to reach its peak in this busy part of the prison complex. Yet, despite this constant traffic of prison officers passing to and fro, the staff is still below strength, a situation aggravated by the nonsensical system that results in up to 50 of the total of 100 discipline staff being away on any one day on escort duties.

During the day girls and women may be employed in their cells, in the workshops or merely on the wing doing nothing in particular. Long-term prisoners are left very much to their own devices and rarely give trouble. It is more likely to be the short-term inmates or Borstal recalls who complain of conditions and who, on various occasions, have sought publicity by demonstrations such as clambering on to the roof. In most cases the attitude of the governor is to let the steam run out of the demonstration by ignoring it, rather than to heighten the tension and publicity-value of the affair by sending officers to bring the girls back. No girl really wants to spend the night on the roof of a cell-block, particularly if nobody is taking any notice of her.

Girls seeking publicity frequently use the quality of prison food as a source of complaint. This is rarely justified, and in any case most of it is cooked by the prisoners themselves. From the writer's own experience in visiting Holloway on many occasions, the food served to prisoners is frequently more appetising and better cooked than that served to the staff.

Despite the apparently casual manner in which inmates of the various wings are supervised, there is no relaxation in the manner in which they are observed and treated. A firm and friendly approach is the ideal, and it is not often that an inmate takes advantage. One of the most serious errors an officer can make is to get herself locked in a cell. This occasionally happens to a trainee who, in the course of inspecting a cell in the absence of the occupant, automatically closes the door behind her. The quiet click that signals the closure is ominous, for there is no keyhole inside and no means of opening the door from within. The highly-embarrassed officer must then try and activate the outside signalling apparatus from within the cell, and endeavour to attract attention by shouting and proclaiming to an interested audience that she is not a prisoner but an officer! This situation, though rare, causes great glee amongst the girls, and is a chastening experience for any officer, as is the reprimand that inevitably follows.

Yet, as happens in most prisons, the visitor to Holloway is immediately impressed by the good relationship existing between staff and prisoners. The image of the prison officer as a rigid disciplinarian, with the prisoner cowed and submissive before her, is completely false yet dies hard. Under modern conditions, despite the grim Victorian buildings, the atmosphere is more pleasant and relaxed than would be thought possible. This is due to the attitude and character of the prison officers, and immediately prompts the question as to what kind of people join the prison service.

While it seems no more odd for a man to become a prison officer than to join the police or armed forces, many people think it slightly unnatural for a woman to join the prison service. Yet it is perfectly natural for a woman to join the service after a period in the army or air force (as many do), and to see in prison work an opportunity for greater self-expression and responsibility than is possible in the forces. For others it means an opportunity of acquiring security and a home of their own; it is noteworthy that some of the best officers are those whose own childhood has been disturbed and unhappy, and who see an opportunity of making life a little easier for those who have got into trouble as a result of their early environment. Some girls who enter the service have always been interested in penology and delinquency, whilst others have come from nursing. Yet so high are the standards that only a third of those applying are accepted.

One odd result of an analysis of reasons why women join the service is that a fairly high number are divorced. The reasons for this can only be guessed at, though a psychiatrist could probably suggest several answers. It may well be that after the tragic experience of a broken marriage, a woman may decide she no longer wishes to live amongst men but prefers feminine company. Whatever her reasons, anyone joining the prison service has undertaken one of the most difficult occupations open to her. It is also one of the most important.

She will soon learn that the hours will be long and, in most prisons, the surroundings grim. She will discover that for most prisoners she will always be one of 'them', with the bunch of keys at her waist a constant reminder that she is the embodiment of discipline and constraint. When she begins her year's probation after training she may find herself working with older officers who have become cynical about the service, and dealing with prisoners who, despite all the help and understanding given them, return to prison again and again and seem incapable of leading normal lives. This first year is the hardest, and it is not surprising that some girls resign then.

But if they can continue, as the majority do, they will soon get past this period of disillusionment. They will find, for instance, that the prison officer who seems most disenchanted with her lot is often the same one who devotes much of her own spare time to shopping for the prisoners and contacting their relatives for them. She will also discover, despite the theories of many penologists, that the prison officer who has the name for being the strictest disciplinarian is also the one who gets most letters from women who leave prison in appreciation of her help and guidance. But for this to happen the officer must be fair in her judgement and always consistent in her attitude. It says a great deal for the service that whatever complaints women make out about imprisonment in Holloway, charges of cruelty or sadism against the officers are rare.

Again, the probationer will come to appreciate that the older prison officer, sometimes a little taciturn and apparently not very helpful, is the one who can be relied upon most in an emergency such as a fight on the wing, or an outbreak of 'smash-ups' in the cells. And as the months go by, to be gradually counted in years, the new officer will discover, as so many have done before her, that despite the difficulties and constrictions of the work, she would never want to do anything else.

The prison officer of today is very much more than a locker-up of cells. She must also be something of a psychologist, trying to understand the prisoners' needs and developing infinite patience. This attitude has been encouraged by the prison authorities and governors since the war and is welcomed by the officers themselves. In some ways, therefore, it is unfortunate that the last few years have seen a marked increase in the number of well-intentioned people visiting Holloway as students and representatives of various organisations, all determined to 'understand' the prisoner and to add their contribution to the millions of words written about delinquency and rehabilitation. In the past their efforts have often overlapped, and despite a certain amount of centralisation there still seems to be an unnecessarily large number of people wanting access to prisoners; in most instances the prisoner does not want access to them.

Some visitors, of course, are essential and welcome, like the chaplains, the various medical authorities and members of the Lady Visitors' Association, which goes back nearly 200 years to the days of Elizabeth Fry. But too many visitors to Holloway give the impression of looking on the inmates rather as a zoologist studies the habits of animals in captivity. The prisoners themselves are peculiarly sensitive to any suggestion that they are 'on show' and resent these intrusions. Said one girl, referring to members of a well-known association, 'The only reason I ever see anybody from there is because of the free cigarettes they dish out.' Some members of associations visiting Holloway do not endear themselves to the staff by their habit of passing to prisoners things that are forbidden by the regulations. Aspirins, for example (all medicine in prison must be taken in liquid form and under supervision), and other items such as materials for weaving or tapestry, which are issued only by the prison officers in charge of that particular course of instruction.

The argument for allowing so many people to visit prisons for sociological studies and contacts with inmates is that, unlike the Lady Visitors and older organisations, they are likely to be younger and may be from the same kind of social background as the prisoner. But in fact many prisoners have indicated that they resent being quizzed by somebody from their own background rather than by someone from an environment they are unlikely to be in after release.

Despite the undoubted 'us' and 'them' attitude of prisoners towards staff, in Holloway most inmates would far rather confide in a prison officer than in any visitor. To the outside visitor a girl will only too often say what she knows is expected. To the officer she will really unburden herself of her hopes and fears, often establishing a bond that lasts long after she is released. But in the articulate and analytical world of today, where the motivation for every action must be revealed and rationalised, the tendency is moving in the opposite direction.

Many prison officers feel that their work would be made even more rewarding if they had greater opportunity of taking courses in psychology and sociology, and that the prisoners would also benefit as a result. But the trend is towards this work being undertaken by specialists in these fields who, despite their training and intellectual capacity, remain strangers and rarely succeed in establishing that bond with the prisoner which is so important. The prison officer today has the uncomfortable feeling that if this tendency continues her function may once more deteriorate to that of a mere locker-up and disciplinarian. This, far more than conditions of pay and employment, is creating resentment and fear amongst prison officers in Holloway.

In the meantime the hierarchy of the Holloway prison system is as follows:

Governor
Deputy governor
Assistant governor (normally one to each wing)
Chief officer (Class 1)
Chief officer (Class 2)
Principal officer
Senior officer

Prison officer
Probationers

In Holloway, since the appointment of Dr Charity Taylor
in 1946, the governor has always been a woman, and in some
cases (as at present) medically qualified in addition. The three
classes of governor are often drawn from outside the prison
service, perhaps from the Home Office or the medical profession, the deputy normally being appointed from one of the
assistant governors. At one time it was rare for a member of
the discipline staff to reach the rank of assistant governor, and
as in the armed forces there were many who did not wish to
attain these heights, preferring to remain in more personal
contact with the prisoners themselves. Now special training
and examinations are available, and any woman joining the
prison service can look forward to reaching the top of the tree
if she is keen enough.

In addition to the discipline staff there are, of course, large
numbers of personnel working in Holloway on many other
duties, including about forty nurses in the hospital and maternity wings, administrative staff, dispensers and pharmacists,
welfare officers, probation officers and others including a small
contingent of men under the Chief Engineer who are responsible for maintenance, and who are joined daily by selected
prisoners from Pentonville, mainly on outside work.

As with the prison officers, there is a chronic staff shortage
in most other sections, largely brought about by attempted
economies in salaries which sometimes prove to be highly
uneconomical. As an example, nursing staff are so poorly paid
that nurses may leave the prison service and register with an
agency—from which they are then hired back to the prison at
a greatly increased salary! The poor pay of pharmacists in
prison and under the National Health Scheme generally leads
to difficulties in obtaining adequate qualified people. The result
is that the control and handling of scheduled poisons and

143

'listed' medicines is often in the care of pharmacy technicians and compounders who, though perfectly capable of doing the work, are not registered pharmacists and are thus breaking the regulations which the Home Office has itself imposed. It is a curiosity that the Pharmaceutical Society, which is required to send inspectors to visit retail pharmacies at frequent intervals to check that the pharmacist is always on the premises, is not permitted to inspect prison dispensaries. In Holloway conditions of work in the dispensary, converted from three cells, are appalling, and it says a great deal for the dedication of the pharmacist and his staff that they perform their work with such efficiency.

Before leaving Holloway as it is today, to look at the prison of the future which is slowly rising on the site, mention must be made of the small and self-effacing organisation which exists to help girls leaving prison to find accommodation and work. This is the Griffins Society, the only society whose sole aim is to help women ex-prisoners to re-establish themselves in the community. It was founded in 1965 and took over the assets of the Holloway Discharged Prisoners' Aid Society, one of thirty-six such societies disbanded on the recommendation of the Advisory Council on the Treatment of Offenders. In 1966 the Society was able to purchase some property in Crowndale Road, Camden Town, and in this unsalubrious and depressing area began work. Two years later, owing to the generosity of Sir Edmund Stockdale, an adjoining property was purchased and the hostel given the name of Stockdale House.

Today the hostel takes thirteen women from Holloway who have no accommodation and no job on release. Some are found employment quickly and stay only a few weeks. Others, perhaps with personality problems, are not so easily dealt with and may stay a year or more. Where possible the residents pay for their board and lodging, but the hostel is to some degree subsidised by the Home Office and receives help from several other organisations including the Greater London Council. Its day-to-day management is in the hands of a capable married couple and under the overall care of a resident secretary who, at the time of writing, is herself an experienced ex-prison officer from Holloway. The supervising committee is formed from people well known in the prison service and includes a psychotherapist who regularly visits the hostel.

Stockdale House is also used to accommodate the families of prisoners in Holloway, and for meetings for families who may have travelled a considerable distance and cannot afford hotel rooms. From the beginning of 1973, as a result of the 1972 Criminal Justice Act, it has also attempted to house girls on remand, who cannot be bailed as they have no fixed abode. The alternative would be a remand in custody, and here the hostel fulfils a particularly useful function. At present it can take only a very few of those who qualify, but it is hoped that further premises may be purchased later.

10

THE NEW HOLLOWAY

Alternatives to Holloway in its present form have been under discussion for over forty years. It has long been obvious that the design of the prison, and of others contemporary with it, is totally unsuited to modern ideas of penology; 'an obstacle to progress in the treatment of women offenders' is how one senior Home Office spokesman has described it.

Yet despite the admission that the majority of British prisons are hopelessly inadequate and out of date, the fact remains that only ten purpose-built closed prisons have been built in this country since Wormwood Scrubs opened its doors a century ago in 1874, with little departure from the original design. Events of national importance such as wars, political crises and economic depressions have militated against this, preference being given to new schools, universities, hospitals and other institutions.

Once again we meet the well-known British habit of pretending an unpleasant situation does not exist by the simple expedient of ignoring it. Whilst this is probably commendable if it results in the 'Dunkirk spirit' which, through the convolutions of the British mind, transforms a thorough trouncing into a resounding victory, it is rather less constructive to attempt to allay the problem of prisons by pushing it to the background for a hundred years.

However, in 1968 James Callaghan, the Home Secretary, announced that the government had at last decided to embark on a programme 'to reshape the system of female penal establishments in England and Wales'. The main feature of this programme would be the demolition and rebuilding of Holloway.

While there was no doubt that the design of Holloway could be greatly improved it was felt that it would be difficult to find a better site. The considerations which applied in 1848 were still valid over a century later. Holloway was convenient for the London magistrates courts from which it drew the majority of its inmates; the cost of finding a suitable site nearer to the centre of London would be prohibitive, and the site was already the property of the Home Office. The difference, this time, was that the new prison would have to be built on the site of the old, and while still allowing it to function, and not on waste land. The problems created by this proviso were immense; such an operation had never before been undertaken in Britain.

To decide the best way in which the matter should be tackled the Prison Department set up a Holloway Project Group, and in July 1968 this organisation began work. The Group included representatives from the many departments of the Prison Service and also from the Department of Health & Social Security. The basic requirements were established, and towards the end of 1969 the Consultant Specialists joined the existing Project Team in an advisory capacity to decide on how best to implement the recommendations of the Group.

The announcement of the redevelopment of Holloway resulted in a flood of advice from interested parties, some of whom, like the Howard League for Penal Reform, had for years been recommending what should be done about the prison system, and whose ideas were welcomed by the Home

Office. Other and newer associations were not backward in adding their own ideas; some, like the Radical Alternatives to Prison (Holloway Campaign Group), though motivated by a genuine desire to improve conditions in prison, tended to weaken their arguments by producing facts and figures which were occasionally inaccurate.

The comparatively small number of women in prison (less than 900 compared with about 36,000 men) at any one time created problems of its own. During the past twenty years women had been gradually removed from their own wings at many provincial prisons, and new penitentiaries provided in existing buildings in various parts of the country.

By the time the decision to rebuild Holloway had been made in 1968 the other establishments for women and girl offenders in England were as follows:

Styal (Cheshire); a closed prison
Exeter; a local prison and closed Borstal.
Askham Grange (Yorks)
Hill Hall (Yorks)   } open prisons
Moor Court (Staffs)
Bullwood Hall (Essex)   a closed Borstal
East Sutton Park (Kent)   an open Borstal
Risley (Lancs)
Brockhill (Worcs)
Pucklechurch (Glos)   } remand centres
Low Newton (Co Durham)

With less than 1,000 women in custody, though it was considered desirable to make visits by families as easy as possible, there were practical difficulties in arranging a large number of small prisons or Borstals spread across the country, though this idea had once been mooted. The plan devised, therefore, was to have a northern and southern group of institutions in existence, each with one closed and one open prison and a closed Borstal (East Sutton Park is likely to remain the only open Borstal for some time) together with various remand centres. Within this scheme the new Holloway will be the closed prison for the south of England and the remand centre for the south-east. It will also provide certain specialist medical and psychiatric services for the whole of the country.

Many considerations were involved in the design of the new Holloway, notably those of security, operational practicability and finance. Many conferences were held to discuss the various aspects of the new prison, some of the most important taking place at Steyning, Sussex. In the event the 'Steyning brief' eventually became the blueprint for the redevelopment of the prison.

The new Holloway embraces two main and fundamental concepts, one of design and the other of function. First, the comment of Dame Lillian Barker that she would prefer to 'imprison women in a park rather than park them in a prison' has been acted upon. Instead of the prison being a 'centre' with cell-blocks radiating outwards from it, the new concept is of living accommodation arranged round the perimeter of the site enclosing a central green campus, virtually turning the present design inside-out.

As to function, bearing in mind that the great majority of women offenders need some form of medical, psychiatric or remedial treatment, and that few are violent or represent a high security risk, it is believed that the new Holloway should be more akin to a hospital than a conventional prison. The Prison Rules, as stated by the Home Office, require that the purpose of the training of convicted prisoners is to encourage them to lead a good and useful life on release.

Therefore the regime at Holloway will have three main themes. First will be immediate assistance to women entering in the matter of family problems, such as provision of meals, meeting children from school and other domestic matters, together with any urgent medical treatment the prisoner may require.

Secondly there will be long-term treatment in various forms, including psychiatric treatment when required, education for the illiterate and backward, and various forms of group counselling and therapy.

Thirdly there is the provision of a community life in prison modelled on life outside which will prepare the woman for coping with a normal existence from the moment she enters Holloway, and which will include tuition in various skills which may augment her income on release, improvement in her ability to communicate, introduction to hobbies which she can pursue in her leisure time, and information as to where she can turn for help in the community if she finds herself in difficulties. It is hoped that by this means she will be taught not only to lead an honest life, but also a reasonably happy one, which so many women who come to prison have never known.

The population of the prison will be roughly as it is at present —between 400 and 500—of whom about one-third will be on remand and awaiting trial or sentence. Free movement around the prison will be allowed with the minimum supervision and escorting of parties from place to place.

Another difference in the treatment of women in prison will be in the categories into which they are divided. No longer will they be grouped according to sentence or offence, but in terms of the treatment they require. Five main units will undertake the various kinds of treatment. First will be a medical and surgical unit for those requiring intensive medical care; an obstetric unit will provide ante-natal and post-natal care together with accommodation for mothers and small children; there will be a psycho-diagnostic unit for treatment of the highly-disturbed or those experiencing the effects of drug addiction or withdrawal; a psycho-therapeutic unit will see to the needs of alcoholics and drug addicts, and finally, there will be a unit for those serving sentences (including Borstal recalls and normal trainees) who are not in need of definite medical treatment but who may benefit from the attention of a psycho-therapist.

In addition there will be an out-patients' department outside the prison providing a full range of clinical services, both to supply medical and psychiatric reports to the courts, and also to provide continuing out-patient treatment for those who require and desire it after release.

The old concept of single 'cells' is, of course, a thing of the past in the new Holloway, and accommodation is provided in single rooms or in dormitories of four beds, all with normal doors and windows. Rooms will be arranged in groups consisting of sixteen beds and two such groups will constitute a section each completely self-contained. Work rooms, the educational block, chapel and offices will be on the furthest side of the prison from the living quarters, 'thus preserving', as David Faulkner has said in the *Howard Journal of Penology*, 'the concept of going out to work'. There is, of course, the consideration that over 100 of the women will not have to work, being on remand, but no mention has so far been made of ways to overcome this problem except to supply them with voluntary work of a kind that can be stopped or taken up again at will.

Mention has been made of the ante-natal care provided in the new prison, and a fundamental change is that women will actually have their confinement in the new Holloway—a reversal of the decision of 1948 which allowed pregnant women to give birth to the child at a local hospital instead of in prison. To many people this is a retrograde step, but the Home Office, with a certain degree of naïveté, considers that the new Holloway will be so like a hospital that no stigma will be attached to having a child there. The maternity ward, in fact, will officially be a ward of the Royal Northern Hospital.

There is even the possibility that the name of Holloway will be changed, though so far no suitable alternative has been found. But however highly the Home Office may rate the new Holloway, to the inmate it will still be a prison, with resultant loss of liberty, whatever the name may be. Nothing will alter this fact, and any woman having a child on the premises will be in no doubt at all that her child was born in prison.

Another change is that, in certain circumstances, mothers will be able to keep their children under the age of five in Holloway with them. Only a few women actually give birth to babies in prison, but many serving custodial sentences have young families left at home. A recent study by the Home Office Research Unit shows that of a sample of 638 women passing through Holloway, 415 had no children but the remaining 223 had 504 children between them, of whom 10 per cent were illegitimate. At present a woman may keep her newborn baby with her until it is two years of age, but she is normally removed from Holloway and transferred to Styal after a few weeks. There she may keep the child until it is two. Under the new scheme accommodation will be provided at Holloway for children up to five years of age whose mothers are serving a sentence and for whom no suitable arrangements can be made outside.

Great importance has been attached to providing good living conditions for the staff at the new Holloway. Both inmates and staff are members of the same community—indeed, the staff will be resident in the prison far longer than most inmates, and this has been taken into account when providing the living quarters.

These have been designed as a series of blocks of flats varying from two to ten storeys, looking out on landscaped areas each separated by a small garden but connected by elevated pathways at the fourth and eighth floors. The blocks are situated on the rising north side of the site, outside the prison, with extensive views over London to the south. Every effort has been made to provide an ambience as natural as is possible in an institutional environment and to bridge the gap between the prison and the surrounding community. An example of this is seen in the play-areas and day nurseries which will be available not only for the children of prison staff but for those of local residents.

Accommodation ranges from units shared by two single staff members to family units with up to four bedrooms. A total of 238 members of the discipline and nursing staff, and their families, will be housed.

The training of staff, which has been proceeding for some time, is centred on a comprehensive programme undertaken both at Holloway and Wakefield which will fit prison officers for the changed duties and attitudes required by the new Holloway. Great attention is being given to the psychiatric approach to offenders, in which group counselling plays an important part, and will include advice and participation from certain specialist organisations such as Alcoholics Anonymous.

Further training will include periods of two or three weeks spent at institutions specialising in psychiatric medicine and therapy such as Broadmoor Hospital, the Maudsley Hospital and Grendon Psychiatric Prison.

It is also likely that in the new Holloway there will be a higher percentage of male prison officers than at present.

By 1980 it is likely that the grim, forbidding entrance-gates of Holloway, the griffons with their gyves and keys, the battlements and turrets and the castellated central tower will be gone for ever. Instead, the new arrival at Holloway will pass through the entrance arch and be greeted by the sight of a green, tree-ringed campus, far from intimidating, surrounded by flat-roofed buildings of two or three storeys and looking far more like a hospital than the prison which it really is. Only in a very few places will there be a perimeter wall to remind inmates of the custodial element of Holloway, for mostly the buildings themselves will form the boundary of the site, thus making maximum use of the space available. The buildings adjacent to the busy Parkhurst Road will be used for administration and will screen the living quarters at the rear from the never-ending roar of traffic at night. The main entrance will be almost on the same spot as the present, immediately adjacent to the complex and traffic-lighted junction of Parkhurst, Camden and Hillmarton Roads.

The new Holloway represents the new concept in the treatment of women offenders—the belief that conventional prisons are unnecessary for the vast majority of women and that their offences are due mainly to personality disorders that will respond to psychiatric treatment. Not everyone agrees with this.

It has been pointed out that the very fact that offences by women are largely trivial, and attract only short sentences, militates against the success of this scheme. No psychiatric treatment that can be of any value can be provided in the three or four weeks that the majority of women prisoners are in custody. If it is unrealistic to expect a woman to learn a new trade in so short a time, it is even less realistic to hope that she will learn a new way of life. To expect that many women will return voluntarily to Holloway for out-patient psychiatric treatment is probably optimistic.

Even from those whose sentences are long enough to gain benefit from this form of therapy there may well be unexpected resistance. For most women in prison the implication of psychiatric treatment is that she has committed an offence and is not fully responsible for her actions, and must be taught by others what is best for her. There are already signs that delinquent women and girls are resenting this suggestion, and seeing in it an unfair discrimination, Men, they are arguing, are not considered mentally wanting if they commit an offence, so why should women be? As they see it, most women who commit crimes, or even minor offences, would certainly prefer to be considered bad than mad—another reason why voluntary attendance at the psychiatric clinic after release is not likely to be very high.

The average prison inmate, as a Home Office Research Unit has said in connection with Borstal detainees, 'can receive little treatment other than the sympathetic rapport, understanding and guidance of the lay staff. This is probably the most important feature of any treatment. . . .' From this it would seem that the vital relationship between prison officer and inmate is at last being recognised, and the usurping of this function by 'trained specialists' from outside might well be disastrous. Whatever success the new Holloway will have in the treatment of offenders, in the final analysis it will depend almost exclusively on the attitude and co-operation of the prison officers, who know their charges and their problems better than anyone else.

Holloway will enjoy a high degree of flexibility for, as the Home Office itself has said in a press-release describing the new prison: 'It is impossible to foresee precisely the likely trends in sentencing policy, but Holloway will still have to receive, accommodate and treat all prisoners sent to it by the Courts.'

This is an important point, for it is the magistrates who determine the sentence and the prison has no power to vary it. Magistrates, who have to listen to the details of offences committed and note the effect on the victims of such offences, are understandably inclined to treat the mugger, the thief, the confidence trickster and the vandal as criminals rather than patients in need of psychiatric treatment. If they decide that a custodial sentence is appropriate they intend it to be a custodial sentence. The Home Office would do well to remember this, and not undermine the sentence of the Courts by embarking on a policy which will transform the status of every criminal into that of a mental defective who is not responsible for his actions.

BIBLIOGRAPHY

Berry, P. and Huggett, R. *Daughters of Cain*, 1956
Buxton, J. and Turner, M. *Gate Fever*, 1962
Carter, M. *A Living Soul in Holloway*, 1938
Crew, A. *London Prisons of Yesterday and Today*, 1933
Crisp, D. *A Light in the Night*, 1960
Croft-Cooke, R. *Bosie—The Story of Lord Alfred Douglas*, 1963
Field, X. *Under Lock and Key*, 1963
Fox, L. *The English Prison and Borstal System*, 1952
Fulford, R. *Votes for Women*, 1957
Hart-Davis, R. *The Collected Letters of Oscar Wilde*, 1962
Henry, J. *Who Lie in Gaol*, 1952
Hinde, R. S. E. *The British Penal System*, 1951
Howard, D. L. *The English Prisons*, 1960
Kelley, J. *When the Gates Shut*, 1967
Klare, H. J. *Anatomy of Prison*, 1960
Lonsdale, K. *et al. Some Account of Life in Holloway*, 1943
McCall, C. *They Always Come Back*, 1938
Mayhew, H. and Binny, J. *Criminal Prisons of London*, 1862
Nield, J. *The State of Prisons*, 1812
Pankhurst, S. *The Suffragette Movement*, 1931
Playfair, G. *The Punitive Obsession*, 1971

Ruggles-Brise, E. *The English Prison System,* 1921
Size, M. *Prisons I Have Known,* 1957
Smith, A. D. *Women in Prison,* 1962
Stern, W. M. *Holloway Prison 1852–1877* (from Studies in London History), 1969
Webb, S. and Webb, B. *English Prisons Under Local Government,* 1922

GOVERNMENT PUBLICATIONS

Criminal Justice Act 1972: *A guide for the Courts,* 1972
Holloway Redevelopment. Prison Dept, Home Office, 1972
People in Prison in England and Wales, 1969
Work for Prisoners. Advisory Council on Employment of Prisoners, 1961
Organisation of the Prison Medical Service, 1964
Studies of Female Offenders. Home Office Research Unit, 1967

ACKNOWLEDGEMENTS

In writing this book I must acknowledge my grateful thanks to the many people, both inside and outside the prison service, who have assisted me with information. Most of all I am indebted to the Home Office itself, which allowed me to write the book, largely as the result of the support of Mrs Joanna Kelley, Assistant Director of Prisons and a former governor of Holloway, and of Mr David Faulkner of the Prisons Department and, at the time, chairman of the Holloway Development Project Group. To both of these I have to acknowledge the use of material taken from their own writings on the subject. In dealing with the new Holloway I must also record the invaluable assistance of the architects concerned, Messrs Robert Matthew, Johnson-Marshall & Partners, in the loan of books and plans.

At Holloway itself I am deeply grateful to the governor, Dr M. P. Bull, for the facilities she allowed me for visiting the prison on many occasions and enabling me to talk freely to staff, probation officers and others, as well as to those serving sentences.

INDEX